WEAVER'S STUDY COURSE

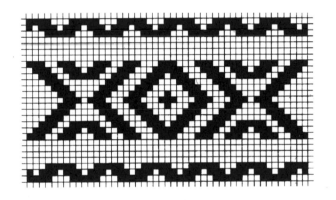

WEAVER'S STUDY COURSE
Ideas and Techniques

ELSE REGENSTEINER

 VAN NOSTRAND REINHOLD COMPANY

NEW YORK CINCINNATI TORONTO LONDON MELBOURNE

ACKNOWLEDGMENTS

Without the splendid cooperation of my weaving friends and students this book could not have been written. They were generous with their work, information, and directions. Their inventive minds and high spirits converted well-known patterns and techniques into new works of art. I wish to thank them all.

Special thanks are due to Hector Garcia for his excellent photography, to Takeko Nomiya for her skillful drafts and to George McVicker for his clear and precise drawings. I appreciate the advice and help of Janet Kravetz in getting this book off the ground and Peter Collingwood's generosity in allowing me to make use of his special techniques.

My deepest gratitude goes to Nancy C. Newman whose skill and knowledge in editing the book could be matched only by her own perception and kindness. My thanks and appreciation also to Judith Vanderwall for her help in preparing the manuscript. Finally I wish to dedicate this book to my husband, whose help and understanding has proved invaluable once again.

COLOR PLATES

Van Nostrand Reinhold Company Regional Offices:
New York   Cincinnati   Chicago   Millbrae   Dallas

Van Nostrand Reinhold Company International Offices:
London   Toronto   Melbourne

Copyright © 1975 by Litton Educational Publishing, Inc.
Library of Congress Catalog Card Number 74-19755
ISBN 0-442-26871-8

Designed by Jean Callan King/Visuality

Published by Van Nostrand Reinhold Company
A Division of Litton Educational Publishing, Inc.
450 West 33rd Street, New York, N.Y. 10001

16 15 14 13 12 11 10 9 8 7 6 5 4 3 2 1

All photographs (unless credited otherwise)
by Hector Garcia.
Drawings by George McVicker.
Drafts by Takeko Nomiya.

Library of Congress Cataloging in Publication Data

Regensteiner, Else, 1906-
    Weaver's study course, ideas and techniques.

    Bibliography: p.
    1. Weaving. I. Title.
TT848.R44   746.1′4   74-19755
ISBN 0-442-26871-8

CONTENTS

INTRODUCTION

This is a book for weavers who are eager to explore new fields but who need stimulation and direction. It is based on my work with study groups of weavers, who found that in working together to solve the problems of a given task they could find new dimensions and challenging solutions well within the bounds of their technical abilities.

The weaving field is bursting with bright young talent. One only has to show a student a new technique and his artistic expression transforms it. One discusses a pattern and immediately imaginative applications come to the student's mind. Such enthusiasm and keen participation are the marks of a good study group. For a weaving course to become a source of ideas, it must be flexible enough to surge like water in a river. A well-known, simple technique may be the source, but it gains with every stream the students add to it, every drop of knowledge, every experiment, every experience.

The return to crafts, with its involvement in basic creative occupations like spinning, dyeing, and weaving, is a search for the source, which has become meaningful as a deep-rooted reaction against our overly technological civilization. Our way of life offers us external ease and a dulling sameness of experience. Yet internal experiences, the joy of life and appreciation of values, can come only from within ourselves. To start from the beginning, taking raw materials and forming them into textiles, for art or function, can never be disillusioning. Each new technique in crafts, each work that expresses its maker is a proof of growing accomplishment.

And there is nothing as rewarding as mastering a new technique and creating exciting accents for one's environment out of design and color, or the satisfaction of weaving a dress in a surprisingly easy way and making the kind of wall hanging that will be accepted in an important show. Imagination and creative spirit can make the simplest technique come alive, and techniques in turn open up possibilities in never-ending variety.

This book is for people who know how to warp a loom and who are familiar with techniques for simple basic weaves. It is meant to be a weaving course that provides general ideas, with clear instructions for carrying them out. It suggests projects without giving precise recipes in order to demonstrate more

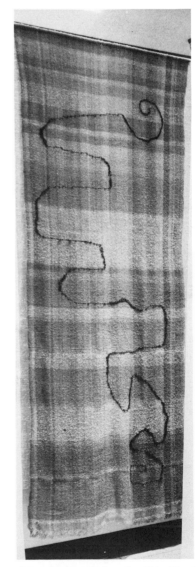

Blue River, wall hanging in mohair and wool by Else Regensteiner; photo by Charles W. Hodge.

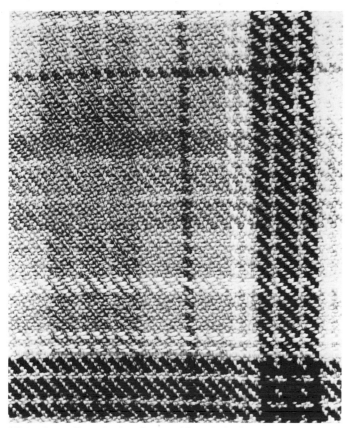

Official Ottawa Tartan by Jean Docton of Canada. It was commissioned by the Centennial Committee of Ottawa in 1966 and put on the market for the opening of Centennial Celebration at 12:01 a.m. January 1st, 1964, on Parliament Hill. Accepted by the City of Ottawa by order of council, the design was designated as the Official Ottawa Tartan. Also shown in color on page 56 (Figure C–17).

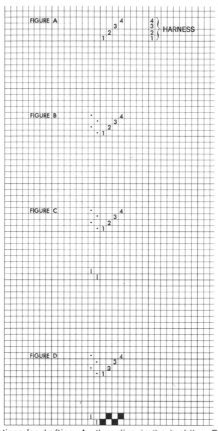

Notations for drafting: A—threading in the heddles; B—tie-up for rising-shed loom; C—sequence of treadling; D—pattern.

NOTATIONS

In order to interpret the drafts the reader should be aware of the symbols used in this book. Threadings (Figure A) are written from left to right. Various weaving books show drafts written from right to left; I find writing from left to right a more natural way. Directions of threadings can, of course, be reversed if preferred.

Filled-in (black) squares in the pattern draw-down (Figure D) represent warp threads which are raised, unless otherwise indicated. All drafts are written for the rising-shed loom. The tie-ups (Figure B) can be reversed for the sinking-shed or counterbalanced loom by tying the opposite harnesses to the treadles. When harnesses 2 and 4 are pulled down the result is the same as if 1 and 3 were raised. Patterns are to be read from the bottom line up.

Color notations are given in the drafts either by symbols or by letters. Keys for notations are placed next to the individual drafts. If variations in symbols are used, they are explained next to the respective drafts.

When large designs are planned, as for rugs, upholstery, or wall hangings, each filled-out square of the graph paper may represent inches or complete threading units instead of the individual threads in the heddles. These diagrams are called short, or profile, drafts because they represent only the relative widths of each pattern block or threading unit.

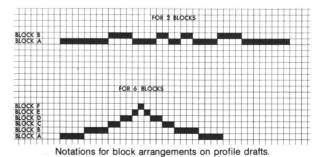

Notations for block arrangements on profile drafts.

general principles. Yet there is enough information to make the execution of each project easy and enjoyable. Throughout, the book shows how to achieve interesting weave effects by interlacing colors and structures and how to apply pattern weaves in new and unusual ways. Many talented weavers have used these weaves and techniques to create joyful, functional, and inspired works of art, and their work is shown here as examples of what can be done by creative weavers. Three-dimensional sculptural hangings are rapidly becoming a more and more integral part of the field of textile construction. It is inevitable, therefore, that work done off loom should be included here. However, it is not within the scope of this book to exhaust any one technique or weave system; the weaver himself is the one to go beyond it in continuing research and to expand his knowledge by seeking out the many books which deal in depth with every technique mentioned in these chapters.

In my first book, *The Art of Weaving,* I was mainly concerned with basic weaves and techniques. Here, I want to expand that knowledge by presenting more advanced weaves, other varieties of techniques, and a fresh new look at the many possibilities inviting exploration. I selected categories pertaining to special areas of interest and chose an extensive variety of problems and projects as stimulation and encouragement for studies. If the reader likes the ideas and suggestions presented in this book, there should be enough material to provide a fertile field for his imagination and to carry him further and further into the functional and creative aspects of textile art.

1 FABRICS FOR CLOTHING

The feel of the handwoven dress, the nearness to the body of the fibers in stoles and wraps, the luscious warmth of glowingly vibrant afghans can produce a joy in clothing and covering which goes beyond vanity or personal adornment. It can be an extension of one's personality and the source of great satisfaction. The product of the human hand has an innate value which no machine-made fabric can convey.

To weave clothing for warmth and for appearance, for feel and for touch, for adornment and for beautification is, perhaps, the most natural beginning of a weaver's study course.

YARNS

Today's weaver is fortunate because sources of yarns have developed to keep in step with the soaring interest in handweaving. From all over the world travelers have brought home news of foreign sources for wools, silks, and linens, and the American mills have accepted the challenge of this competition, adapting to new ideas and suggestions. Handspinners are at work not only for their own satisfaction and supply, but also to follow the ever-growing demand of the handweaver.

The pendulum has been swinging back, gradually but unmistakably, to a new appreciation of handweaving among the general public. The very special handwoven woolen fabric created for a suit, the lovely stole bought at a local art fair, the brilliantly patterned skirt, and the rough, simple, and stunning poncho are familiar products of the contemporary clothing scene. To create these clothes, wools from black, brown, and cream-colored sheep in their natural shades, or yarns dyed in brilliant arrays of colors in every hue and tint, can be found in many specialized weaving shops or may be ordered by mail from generous sample cards. They can even be bought in department stores supplied by an understanding and imaginative buyer. A new interest in plant dyeing has resulted in beautiful soft and mellow colors that at one time were seen only in primitive or ancient textiles.

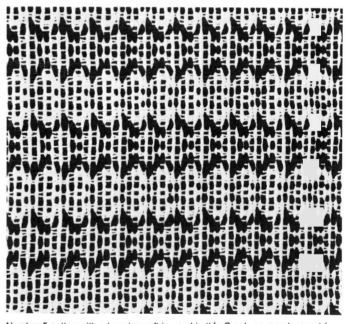

Number 5 cotton with a heavier weft is used in this Greek-woven placemat (see Figure 4–22).

For a textile craftsman, there is nothing like the excitement generated by a colorful abundance of yarns in many weights, textures, and fibers. Not every weaver has the opportunity to find these yarns in one store, but every weaver can, little by little, collect yarns in small amounts—here a ball and there a skein—until a variety is on hand for samples whenever the urge to weave arises. There is not a length of thread which sooner or later could not be just the special little touch needed in a piece. The lack of a large selection of yarns should never prevent the weaver from planning and starting to weave. With imagination, knowledge, and judgment of quality, nearly any thread can be made to perform.

The principal requirement for a warp yarn is tensile strength which usually implies a firm twist. The tensile strength can be determined easily by a quick sharp pull on the yarn between the two hands. If it breaks, the yarn is not strong enough to withstand the great pressure to which a warp is subjected. The texture of a good warp yarn should not be so fuzzy that the threads stick together between heddles, impeding the movement of the reed. When yarns are thick and heavy, the warp setting must be carefully considered, and the weaver must choose spaces wide enough to permit the threads to be beaten without causing undue abrasion and friction.

For weft, yarns do not have to be as strong, so they can be of looser twist. For this reason almost anything available can be adapted to suit the weaver's purpose. When threads are too fine, they can be doubled or tripled on the shuttle or plied together. They also can be manipulated for unusual textural effects: weft yarns can be used in unspun condition, or can be re-spun, unraveled, or knotted. It is possible in this way for the weaver to create yarn textures which will transmit his concepts and express his ideas of surface treatment to perfection.

Wool, cotton, and metallic copper threads create a striking blend for an upholstery fabric (see Figure 3–5).

SAMPLES

The planning of a piece of clothing can be approached in two different ways. The weaver can experiment with yarns, patterns and weaves, reed settings, and techniques, and from among these samples select a project to be woven. Or he can plan a definite project first, and progress to the selection of yarns, settings, techniques, and weaves according to the function of the piece. Either approach requires the weaver to make samples.

Samples are a basic necessity in weaving. Nothing valuable, and certainly no suitable fabric, can come from happy ignorance. Making samples is exciting, and many weavers find it the most rewarding part of weaving. Discovering, conceiving, creating, and finally testing yarns, settings, threadings, and treadlings—and all in many themes and variations—this is the basis for the success of the final piece.

Samples are important not only for the creative but also for the practical approach. They enable the weaver to try out many different yarns, to avoid errors of judgment, and to estimate correctly the amount of yarn needed for the project, as explained in basic weaving books.

A weaver should not follow recipes step by step and thread by thread, for this leads to predictable but imitative results; instead, some general guidelines to sampling will be given here as assistance and encouragement.

Fabric

To weave a good fabric for clothing, the yarn size must be selected according to weight and the eventual function of the material. The fabric may become a suit, coat, dress, skirt, man's sportcoat, or a heavy item such as a poncho or cape. Use the weight or count of a wool yarn as a general guideline to the proper setting. The size of a yarn can best be judged by the number of yards in a pound; the finer the yarn is spun, the more yards are contained in a pound.

Fine wool or worsted yarns averaging 4,000 to 5,000 yards per pound should be set 24 to 30 threads, or ends, per inch. This is yarn of approximately a 16/2 to 18/2 count. Tweed yarns, averaging 2,400 to 3,600 yards per pound, are successfully set from 15 to 24 ends per inch. Four-ply knitting yarns, which average from 500 to 600 yards per pound, can be used for scarves, blankets, and ponchos with a sleying of 10, 12. 15, or 18 threads per inch. Bulky yarns, such as Swedish rya, heavy mohairs, and some handspuns can be set loosely at 8 threads per inch. Attractive lightweight stoles may be woven in fine wool of a 16/2 or 18/2 count and spaced in the reed by doubling, tripling, or skipping in the dents. Of course, for attractive textural effects various kinds of yarns can be combined.

Warp and Weft

A good warp, useful for sectional warping, is one selected to be used with 45 spools per 2-inch section. The threads can then be sleyed alternately single then double in a 15-dent reed.

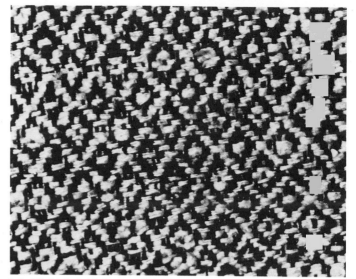

1-1. Silk fabric in bird's-eye twill by Else Regensteiner.

Always use a coarse reed for wool yarns rather than a fine one. To avoid streaks, the threads should be evenly distributed in the dents.

In a good piece of clothing fabric the weft and warp are so well blended that it is difficult to distinguish them without careful examination. The weft can be the same size as the warp but quite varied in texture. If, however, pattern is important, as, for instance, in the effects achieved by the combination of color and weave, yarns of the same size and texture are needed in warp and weft.

Fabrics for clothing can be in all one color, all one texture, or a combination of colors and textures. Stripes are sometimes more successful when laid in the warp than in the weft. Twills and twill variations can be made in great variety, and frequently the simplest threadings and treadlings give the most satisfactory results.

Finishing

Samples should always be tested by proper finishing. If a sample is all wool, it can be washed and pressed to determine its shrinkage and any change in density and appearance. It should be noted that the wool fabric will be tighter after finishing than it was on the loom. Samples also are tighter and closer in weave when woven in narrow instead of wide widths. These facts must be given consideration when the number of warp and weft threads are determined on the loom; otherwise a fabric may become too bulky and heavy to be tailored successfully.

Fabrics in fibers such as silk, cotton, linen, and synthetics shrink differently than wool, or may not shrink at all, so the finishing process often need consist only of dry cleaning and steam pressing by a good professional cleaner. Spot-resisting finishes such as Scotchgard can be applied at the same time. Blends and mixtures should also be treated this way.

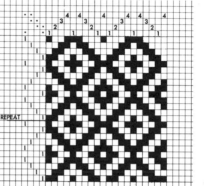

1-1a. Draft.

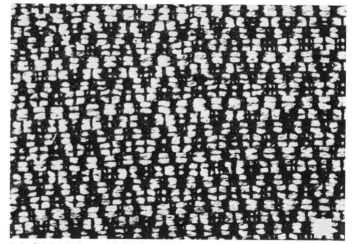

1-2. Silk fabric for coat in herringbone twill by Else Regensteiner.

PATTERNS BASED ON TWILL THREADINGS

One of the most basic, useful, and attractive patterns for clothing fabrics is twill. The diamond or birds-eye twill (Figure 1-1) is easy to thread and easy to weave, and the effect is pleasing whether it is used for a man's silk jacket or in a woman's suit. The material is treadled as drawn in (which means treadling in the same order as the warp was threaded in the heddles). This treadling order can be followed in any kind of twill tie-up.

A bolder pattern, which is very effective for an all silk or a wool-silk coat material, can be woven on the same warp and threading, but using the silk tripled on the shuttle and adding a black tabby (Figure 1-2). The tabby is used single on another shuttle. To enlarge the design, each pattern pick is repeated, with alternating tabby picks between each of them. This is treadled:

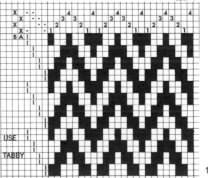

1-2a. Draft.

1–2 (for pattern, use gray silk triple on shuttle)
Tabby A (1–3) (black silk)
1–2
Tabby B (2–4) (black silk)
2–3
Tabby A
2–3
Tabby B
3–4
Tabby A
3–4
Tabby B
4–1
Tabby A
4–1
Tabby B
Repeat from start.

When the small bird's-eye pattern is used as a 1/3 twill (one warp raised and three covered by the weft), a pleasantly textured all-over pattern results on one side. Most of the weft yarn is on the surface. The other side shows mainly the warp. In Figure 1–3 this pattern is shown in a warp arrangement of three colors (moss green, orange, and gold wool), and the softly striped effect makes the fabric attractive on both sides.

1–4. Dress fabric on six harnesses by Takeko Nomiya.

Weaving a dress material with a lengthwise pattern band in the front panel (Figure 1–4) can be easily done when six harnesses are available for this project. Any pattern which does not require a tabby between the pattern picks can be threaded on the last four harnesses, while the first two harnesses are used for the plain weave sections. Color variations may be added, but are not necessary. The same system can be applied on eight harnesses, where other weave combinations or more variations may be desired.

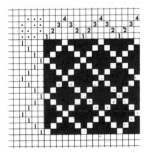

1–3. Fine wool fabric in bird's-eye twill (reversed, 3/1) by Nancy Gardner Miller.

1–4a. Draft for panel pattern.

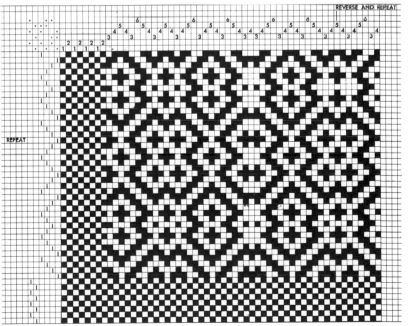

1–3a. Draft.   1–3b. Variation: draft for 1/3 bird's-eye twill.

Fabrics of heavier and sturdier construction than in any other method can be produced by double weaves. One example is a reversible coat fabric woven on eight harnesses, one side showing a mixture of rich brown wools, the other side a combination of textured natural yarns (Figure 1–5). The warp for this fabric is set 30 threads per inch in a 15-dent reed. The alternating light and dark threads are sleyed together in each dent. Note that light and dark threads alternate in the weft also and that the interlacing is planned so that no threads of one layer are visible on the surface of the other layer, although the double weave is connected, or "stitched," and can not be separated as in tubular weaves. The threads which connect the two layers can be *risers,* threads raised from the bottom layer to interlock with the top. Threads from the top layer can be lowered to interlace with the bottom layer and are therefore called *sinkers.* When such a fabric is planned, it must be arranged so that the backing weft threads slide under those in the preceding and following row and are hidden between them. The two examples in Figures 1–5b and c demonstrate good and poor arrangements.

Twill patterns can also be made on eight harnesses. With the additional harnesses, more intricate designs can be made, but a limitation of texture and color is necessary to show the construction of the weave to the fullest effect. Patterns which depend on the weave structure show most clearly when warp and weft are in contrasting colors, and when the variation of yarn textures is kept at a minimum.

1–5. Coat fabric with double-weave backing by Lurene K. Stone.

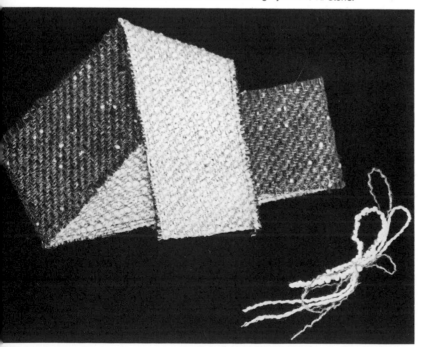

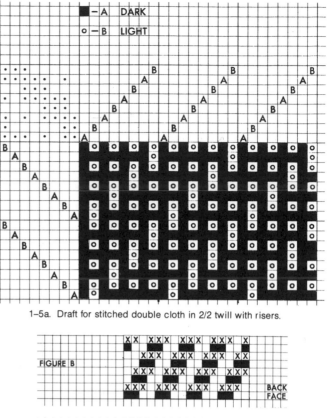

1–5a. Draft for stitched double cloth in 2/2 twill with risers.

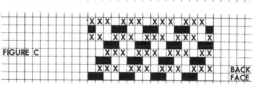

1–5b and c. Two drafts demonstrating good and poor backing arrangements. In the good example (b) the back filling stitches lie under floats. In the poor example (c) there are back filling ridges to the top.

For the fabric shown in Figure 1–6, an extremely fine mercerized cotton thread, size 50/3, is set, doubled, at 48 threads per inch in a 24-dent reed. The fineness of the thread, used in both warp and weft, makes a lovely, soft, closely woven material. The black warp, woven with a weft of bright colors, brings out clearly the traces of this interesting eight-harness twill. A size 40 or other fine sewing thread could be used instead of mercerized cotton.

1–6. Skirt material woven in very fine cotton thread by Geraldine Wood.

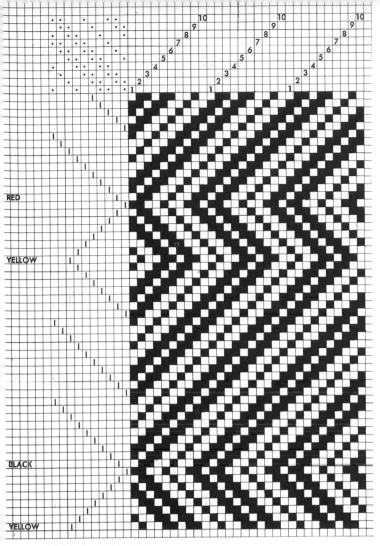

RED

YELLOW

BLACK

YELLOW

1–6a. Draft for twill stripe.

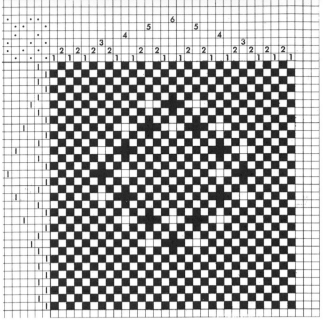

1–7a. Draft.

PATTERNS BASED ON COLOR INTERLACEMENT

Surprisingly striking effects can be achieved by interlacing colors in warp and weft. The design is based on sequences of colors in the warp, which are repeated in the weft to produce many different patterns depending on the weave. Plain weave can make the well-known log-cabin (Figure 1–8) and shepherd's check patterns, but twill combinations in simple threadings often result in very intricate-looking fabrics for clothing.

The same kind of thread was used in Figure 1–7 in a blue-green combination by the same weaver. It has a setting of 48 threads per inch but combines plain weave and lace spots on six harnesses. These can be distributed by the weaver as desired.

1–7. Dress material in fine cotton thread by Geraldine Wood.

1–8. Coat fabric in brown and natural wool in log-cabin pattern by Else Regensteiner.

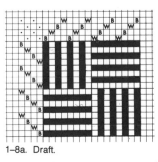

1–8a. Draft.

13

CHECKS AND TARTANS

Checks and tartans, which came from Scotland, have been used in their original color arrangements or in contemporary interpretations since they became widely popular early in the nineteenth century. Most handweavers are well acquainted with these designs and have woven many of them in the traditional color schemes or their own variations (Figure 1–9). How interesting such a project can be is illustrated in color on page 56 (Figure C–17). It starts from a basically traditional design by the Canadian weaver, Jean Docton, which was designated in 1967 as the official tartan of Ottawa. The sequence in the warp and weft stripes is the same. It is as follows in number of threads:

red - 4	white - 4
gold - 24	gold - 4
white - 4	white - 4
gold - 4	gold - 24
white - 4	white - 8
gold - 4	gold - 28
navy - 8	azure blue - 16
gold - 4	gold - 4
navy - 12	azure blue - 16
gold - 4	gold - 4
navy - 8	azure blue - 16
gold - 4	gold - 28

The symbolism of the colors is:

Three navy stripes—(1) Royal engineers who built the Bytown Canal as a means of defence and transportation. (2) Samuel Chaplin, first explorer of the area. (3) Outacuais Indian tribe, from which Ottawa gets its name.

Three azure stripes—The three rivers that intersect at the Capital building, (1) Ottawa River, (2) Gatineau River, (3) Rideau River.

White stripes—The white pine that was the reason for Ottawa being founded at the intersection of the rivers.

Gold stripes—Royal assent making Ottawa the capital of Canada.

Red stripe—Capital buildings situated at the intersection of the three rivers.

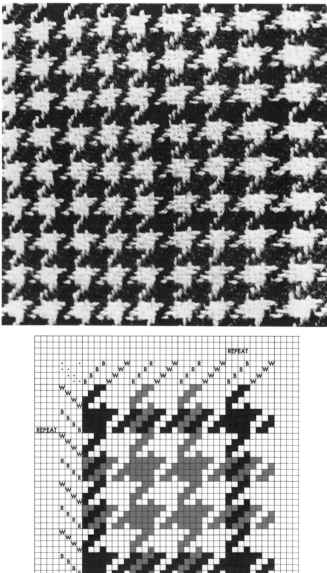

1–9. Window-pane check (houndstooth) fabric woven in 2/2 twill.

1–9a. Draft. Color B is black; W is white; R is red.

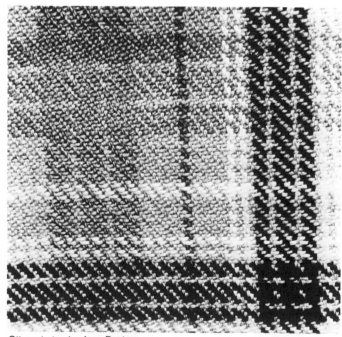

Ottawa tartan by Jean Docton

COLOR-AND-WEAVE EFFECTS

Some interesting examples of color-and-weave effects are shown in Figures 1–10 to 1–15. The drafts are self-explanatory and work very well for any kind of clothing material. Note carefully the variations in the threading sequences. So many designs can be created by changes in threading sequence that a weaver will be well repaid by a careful study of the effects of threading. The caftan in black and white yarns (Figure 1–16) is an excellent example. Both warp and weft are a fairly heavy acrylic sport yarn that does not pucker. It is sleyed in the reed at 12 threads per inch. The color-and-weave effect is very striking, and the uncluttered lines of the garment emphasize the interesting fabric resulting from threading, color, and treadling combinations.

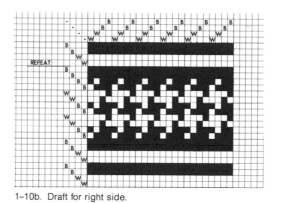

1–10b. Draft for right side.

1–10. Color-and-weave effect in fabric woven in 1/3 twill.

1–11. Color-and-weave effect in fabric woven in 2/2 twill.

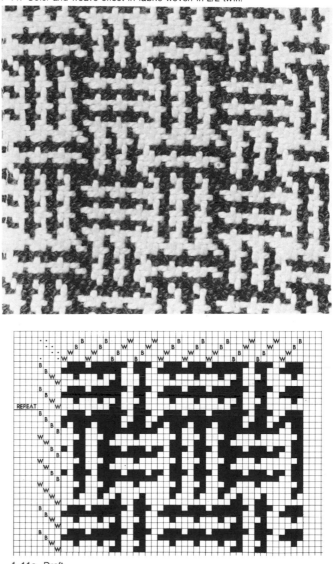

1–10a. Reverse side.

1–11a. Draft.

15

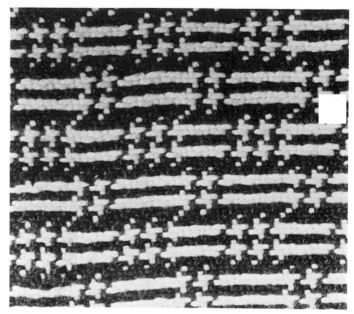

1–13. An interesting variation in color-and-weave effect. Compare the changes in threading with those in Figure 1–10.

1–12. Variation of color-and-weave effect, woven in 1/3 twill.

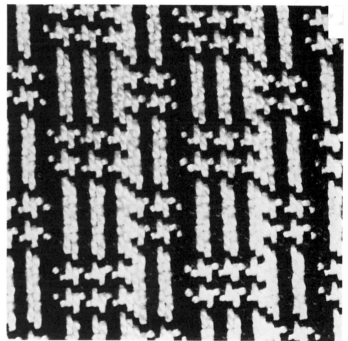

1–13a. Reverse side.

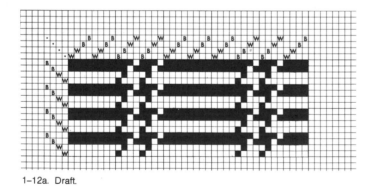

1–12a. Draft.

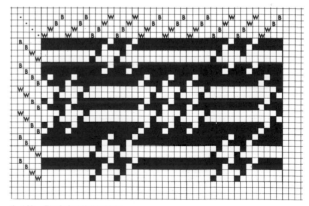

1–13b. Draft for right side.

1–14. In this color-and-weave variation the threading pattern was also changed.

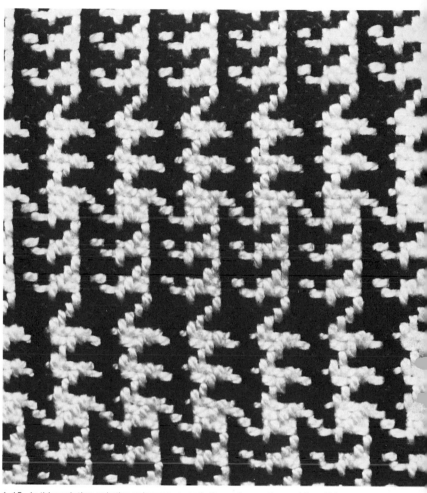

1–15. In this variation only the color sequence in the weft was changed from the arrangement in Figure 1–14. Warp and threading remained the same.

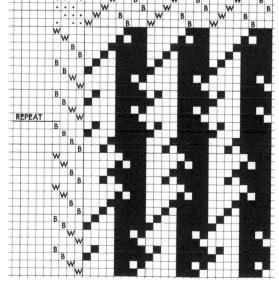

1–14a. Draft.

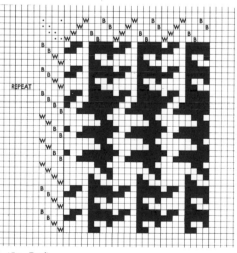

1–15a. Draft.

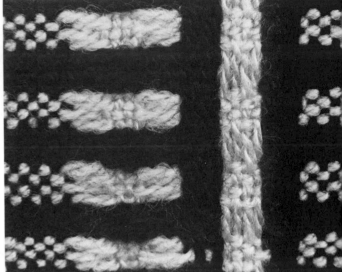

1–16a. Detail.

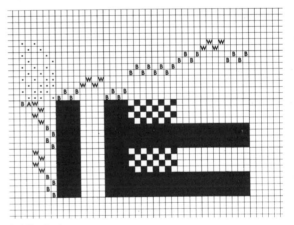

1–16b. Draft.

1–16. Black-and-white caftan in color-and-weave effect by Marjorie O'Shaughnessy; photo by Mark Rychek.

PATTERNS BASED ON VARIOUS WEAVES AND COMBINATIONS

Satin Weave

Satin weave has been traditionally used mainly for very fine fabrics such as brocades and damasks. Intricate designs, which can be traced from the Middle Ages through the nineteenth century, were made by handloom action on the draw loom. This complicated and sensitive loom allows for the lowering and raising of individual warp threads in any combination. It probably came from the Orient to the West with the first introduction of silk into the Western world and its development through many centuries led to the invention of the mechanically operated Jacquard loom, which is instrumental in the production of most of our power-loomed, complicated, patterned textiles. The basic methods in brocades and damasks (Figure 1–17), especially the satin weave, can be explored successfully by the contemporary handweaver. The satin weave, which serves as the basic structure for many of the fine traditional fabrics, can be simplified and converted to contemporary use. Satin weave, as used in a wool cape (Figure 1–18) produces very interesting results. The weave makes a definite warp- and weft-faced material, both of which were combined in the cape to great advantage.

The detail of the warp satin fabric shows a five-end satin, the minimum number of harnesses needed for a true satin structure. Satin differs from a twill structure by the distribution of the points of interlacement between warp and weft. In satin weave these points do not overlap or even touch each other, and cause relatively long floats in warp or weft. Definite sides of either warp-faced or weft-faced surfaces are characteristic of this weave. The diagonal twill line, although actually present, usually is not distinguishable in very fine, closely set and closely woven satin fabrics. As mentioned, regular satin weaves repeat on as low as five ends or threads.

In order to construct a satin weave one can apply the following method. A counter (also called a base) is used in a mathematical way to find the interlacement points of warp and weft. This counter is found by separating the number of threads in the repeat (e.g., five for a five-harness satin) into two parts. These two parts *cannot* be equal, *cannot* have number 1 as one of their components, must *not* have a common divisor with each other or with the total number, and must *not* be a multiple of each other. Therefore, an eight-end satin could be constructed with the help of counter 3 or 5, but *not* with one of 2 or 4, since these numbers divide evenly into 8.

For a five-end satin a counter of either 2 or 3 can be used. A nine-end satin is possible with counter 2, 4, 5, or 7 but not with a 3 or 6.

The first step in designing a satin weave must be the determination of a correct counter. When the weave is drawn on graph paper, the first square in the lower left-hand corner is filled out, representing the first warp end to interlace with the first weft pick.

1–17. Satin damask cloth, France, first half of 17th century; photo courtesy of the Art Institute of Chicago.

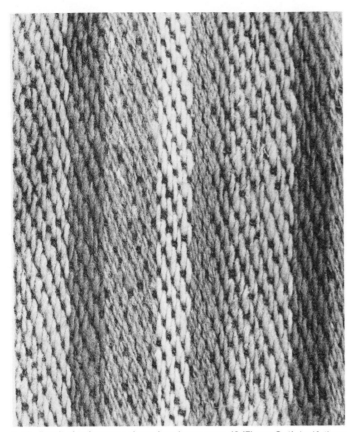

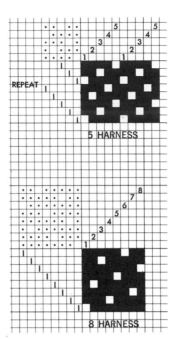

1–18. Detail of satin weave shown in color on page 49 (Figure C–1), by Kathryn Wertenberger. This is the warp satin on the right side.

1–18b. Draft of warp satin.

1–18a. Detail showing reverse side in weft satin.

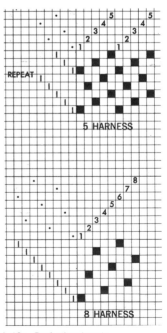

1–18c. Draft of weft satin.

For the next step, the counter is used. The counter number is added to number 1 (the first interlacing point) to determine the second pick. This method is continued until a repeat is reached, thus completing the weave construction. The formula can be written out in an easily understandable fashion. For a five-end satin (which makes the number 5 the limit of the repeat), using counter 2:

    1 plus 2 is 3
    3 plus 2 is 5
    5 plus 2 is 7; 7 minus 5 is 2
    2 plus 2 is 4
    4 plus 2 is 6; 6 minus 5 is 1

With the arrival at number 1 the repeat has been found (see Figure 1–18c). The whole sequence of picks (1–3–5–2–4) repeats itself for the width of the warp. Many variations of regular and irregular satin weaves can be constructed on this principle. The explanation, which describes the most convenient way I have found to find the proper counter, is not the only method, but is meant to encourage the reader to explore for himself the limitations and possibilities of satin weave.

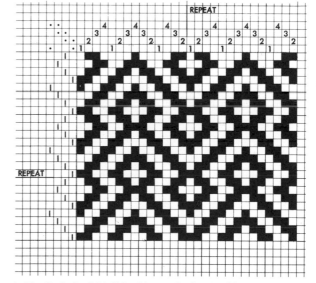

1–19a. Draft for Summer-and-Winter pattern in lower panel of skirt by Barbara De Peaux, shown in color on page 53 (Figure C–10)

COMBINATIONS OF TECHNIQUES

The most imaginative clothing can be made with combinations of techniques such as knitting, stitchery, pattern weaves, and tapestries. The skirt shown in color on page 52 (Figure C-9), is woven in plain tubular weave, embroidered with designs of reindeer and flowers, and adorned with crocheted balls. The belt is woven separately. Colors in the skirt are repeated in the sweater in a tapestry-like knit design with embroidered patterns in wools and mohairs. The warp in this charming skirt is a pale green rayon, set at 10 threads per inch and woven with alternating white and aqua cotton threads. Flowered ribbon is appliqued to the woven background, twisted to reveal both the controlled flower pattern and the abstract qualities of the reverse side. Human forms, deer, birds, and flowers are embroidered on the woven surface. Large, multicolored crocheted balls are sewn to the skirt.

The sweater was knitted in one piece with colored background areas, human figures, deer, geometric designs, hearts, and multicolored popcorn stitch all included in the knitting. Only the birds and flowers were embroidered on the knit surface, and the larger crocheted balls sewn on. In Figure C–10 on the next page, the same artist has used a very interesting and imaginative combination of patterns and techniques. In this skirt, the front and back panels are done in free-form tapestry technique, following an exact drawing made ahead of time. Side panels and waist band are woven in the point-twill pattern (Figure 1–19b), which is loom controlled, and the lower skirt panel was threaded to a Summer and Winter draft (Figure 1–19a).

1–19b. Draft of point twill in side panels of same skirt.

Summer and Winter is a versatile pattern; you will find it in many other fabrics in this book. Basically a block weave, it can take many forms and shapes. Variations in treadlings, proportions, and color arrangements, together with many changes in threading potentials make this pattern extremely useful.

To bring forth the dramatic impact and beauty of hand-woven fabrics, uncluttered classical lines in the garment are

most effective. An excellent example is illustrated in Figure 1–20. It is a tubular weave of hand-dyed perle cotton, sizes 3 and 5, and is made in one piece. The only trim is cotton yarn, plaited into flat bands to frame the neck and sleeves. At the neck they extend into a tie at the throat; at the sleeves, the ends are used to tie the sleeves together.

The equally dramatic dress in Figure 1–21 was woven by the same artist in a herringbone point-twill pattern in separate panels. Each panel is a different color: red, yellow, blue, green, and maroon. The center sections of the front and back of the dress have sets of square and half-hitch knots inserted at the knee. Neck and sleeves are also edged in lengths of square knots, and finished at the neck with large wooden beads. The sleeves are woven as one piece, emphasizing the diagonal lines of the dress panels. In this dress, the weaver uses a wool-mohair blend yarn for warp and Scottish wool for the weft.

Cardweaving and Other Techniques

Other techniques shown on page 50 (Figures C–2, C–3, and C–5) are rya knots inserted in a wool vest of plain weave during the weaving to make a warm furlike trimming, a skirt made of cardwoven and inkle-woven strips, and a belt fashioned from a single cardwoven strip. The technique of cardweaving has recently been explored for many purposes, functional as well as decorative. A discussion of this fascinating method of weaving will be found in Chapter 2, along with more details on other small-loom techniques.

Woven skirts like that in Figure C–3 would be decorative even when hung on a wall. The frequency with which well-designed and executed items could be switched from the decorative to the functional, and vice versa, is one of the most intriguing aspects of the weaver's art.

The great scope and variety possible in clothing fabrics should be stimulating to any weaver, may he or she be in a seriously practical mood or have the urge to combine threads for a lighthearted, colorful, quickly woven project.

1–20. Tubular dress by Dona Rosenblatt; photo by Richard Schultz.

1–21. Dress in herringbone fabric by Dona Rosenblatt; photo by Richard Schultz.

2 CLOTHING ACCESSORIES

Imagination plays a main role in designing and weaving accessories for clothing such as ponchos and vests, scarves and stoles, collars, and jewelry. More than in the sober suit and coat materials, techniques, colors, and fibers can be combined to give unusual effects to accessories. Even simple projects can be expressions of playfulness and love of decoration.

TUBULAR WEAVES

Many garments and accessories shown in this book were woven in tubular fashion on the loom. Therefore a short explanation of this useful method of weaving should be helpful in understanding the simple procedure and in stimulating the reader to weave his or her own original creations.

Tubular weaves are double weaves—two layers of fabric are woven one on top of the other and joined at both edges. The tubular weave can be made on any warp which is threaded to a twill (Figure 2–1a), but the weaver must consider that there will be twice as many warp threads as for a single layer. A tubular weave with few warp threads for each layer may be woven as a weft-faced material, but for a warp-and-weft combined fabric, the warp threads must be doubled. The hollow tube is made by the treadle arrangement. The shuttle carries the weft thread across the top layer and then around and back across the bottom layer, or vice versa, and connects the edges of the top and bottom layers on both sides (Figure 2–1b). Make sure that the warp consists of an uneven number of threads, so that the weave continues in a regular interlacement without mistakes at the edges. Also, to keep the joined edges from becoming too tight, the first and last three dents in the reed are sleyed with only one thread, while the main part is sleyed with two threads in each dent. Threading in the heddles, however, remains single all the way through.

2–1. Party poncho by Jean Stamsta; photo courtesy of the artist.

2–1a. Draft for a closed tubular double weave.

2–1b. Diagram of a closed tubular double weave.

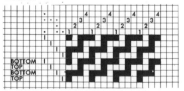

2-2. Jean Stamsta at the loom; a Milwaukee Sentinel Photo.

The same weaver wove the two winter coats in Figures 2–3 and 2–4. The coat in Figure 2–4 was made in tubular weave in warm colors—red, orange, and magenta. As shown in this coat, tubular weaves need not always be completely round. Instead of going around and around, the shuttle reverses directions at the center of the top layer, thus creating an opening (Figure 2–4a).

2-3. *Winter Coat for +0° Fahrenheit,* tubular double weave by Jean Stamsta; photo courtesy of the artist.

2-4. *Winter Coat for −0° Fahrenheit,* by Jean Stamsta; photo courtesy of the artist.

PONCHOS AND COATS

A minimum of sewing is required when a garment is shaped on the loom. In a poncho for instance, a tubular weave can be made with slits for neck and arm openings, following a precut paper pattern. No limit can be set to the range of variations with which fringes, tapestry weaves, rya knots, stripes, and plaids can be used. The colorful party poncho in Figure 2–1 is made in wools and synthetics by combining tapestry weaves with pompons of rya knots. Woven in one piece, it is similar to designs one sees in Guatemalan blouses. The neck is made by weaving a slit, twice as long as the vertical opening will be, in the center of the piece. The sides are completely straight and can be sewn together or left open.

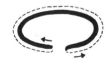

2-4a. Diagram of a tubular weave open in front, such as the coat.

2–5. Fringed vest of brown and gray wools by Dona Rosenblatt; photo by Richard Schultz.

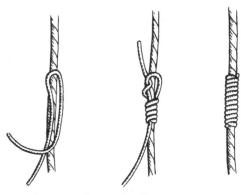

2–5a. Three steps in wrapping fringes.

In contrast to the tubular coats, the vest in Figure 2–5 was woven in three pieces, of heavy wools in browns and grays. In addition to the Ghiordes-knot fringes around the lower third of the vest, unspun alpaca was laid in horizontally in other areas and fringes of it left for decoration. The vertical fringe at the bottom was finished by an interesting wrapping of groups of the warp yarns.

Wrapping

Sometimes weavers wonder how to wrap warp threads without showing knots or having to tuck in the ends with a needle. Figure 2–5a shows a method well known to girl scouts and boy scouts. Fold the wrapping yarn in a loop and lay it parallel on the warp group you intend to wrap. Hold tightly and start wrapping from the bottom up with one length of the looped yarn. When you reach the top, put the end of the wrapping yarn through the loop and pull the other end of the loop downwards. The loop and the free end at the top both disappear inside the wrapping and make a very neat finish. The long end at the bottom can be clipped. The same method can be used in reverse when the wrapping is planned to start from the top.

STOLES, SCARVES, AND MUFFS

One can weave simple lengths of material into long and luxurious stoles, which then can be draped in any way according to the mood of the wearer. Soft fabrics in mixtures of mohair and wool, woven in beautiful blends of colors on warps which are not sleyed very closely—as few as 8 or 10 threads per inch—make stoles which are warm and pleasing to the touch. A soft beat for the weft, to make the material light and airy, is of utmost importance.

More formal scarves, in intricate color patterns, can also include several weaves joined together like a tapestry. The scarf in Figure 2–6 is woven lengthwise on the loom, with the central panel interlocking with the side sections in tapestry fashion. The colors of the side sections are black and white; the center section, threaded in a different pattern, is red and turquoise.

The party muff shown in color on page 54 (Figure C–12), shows a great deal of imagination. The tubular woven body of the muff is decorated with colorful woven bands and wrapped ropes (Figure 2–7), making this muff not only a functional object, but also a charming work of art.

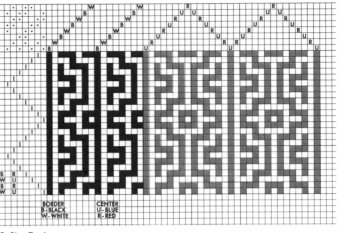

2–6b. Draft.

2–6. Scarf in pattern weave by Jane MacRae.

2–6a. Detail.

2–7. Diagram for party muff by Barbara De Peaux, shown in color on page 54 (Figure C–12).

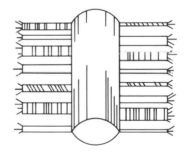

BAGS

Woven bags can be made in many different ways. The one I like is a Greek tagari (pronounced *tahari*) bag, made in one strip and folded to create a simple pocket-type bag which usually has a twisted yarn handle added later (Figure 2–8). It is woven so that the "embroidery" is folded back to form a decorative edge. This specific technique is actually not embroidery at all, but decorative weaving on the loom with the underside facing the weaver. The areas of color are laid in with small butterflies or just a length of yarn according to a design worked out first on graph paper. The shed is closed and the warp threads, represented on the graph by the filled-in squares (Figure 2–8a) are picked up with a stick or the fingers. Then the weft thread is inserted underneath. Since the design areas are small and new strands of color are needed often, the weft is inserted in such a way that the beginning of the thread is carried around a warp thread, as shown in Figure 2–8c. The loose ends of the threads should also be doubled back.

Next, the shed is opened and a tabby is thrown from selvage to selvage. These steps are repeated for the length of the design. The rest of the bag is in plain weave. It is finished with knotted fringes of the weft wool and handsomely twisted or braided handles. The diagrams here show the folding of the woven bag and how it is sewn together at the sides with sewing thread.

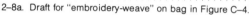

2–8a. Draft for "embroidery-weave" on bag in Figure C–4.

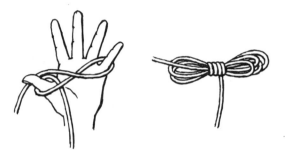

2–8b. Winding butterfly for "embroidery weave."

2–8c. Starting in-laid thread for "embroidery weave."

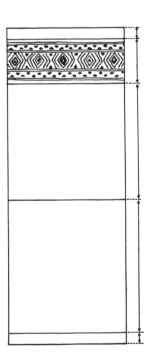

2–8. Diagram for tagari bag shown in color on page 50 (Figure C–4).

2–8d. Folding of tagari bag.

BELTS (INKLE WEAVING)

Weavers who do not work on large looms have wide scope for making accessories in the use of card and inkle looms, finger weaving, and braiding. These techniques are frequently appreciated because they are both versatile and portable; such compact looms can be taken anywhere.

Inkle weaving

Basic inkle weaving is done on a loom consisting of a wooden frame with several stationary and one adjustable dowel (Figure 2–10a, no. 7) that controls the tension of the warp. The shed is made with the help of string heddles, which the weaver can make. The diagrams show how each thread, which has been measured and cut to the desired length of the belt, is put on the loom individually in a continuous wrapping. Its ends are knotted together so that the warp can rotate freely. The width of the band depends on the number of warp threads. In threading the loom, only alternating threads are pulled through string heddles. The other threads are not in heddles at all. To make one shed, the warp threads without heddles are pressed down by hand (Figure 2–10b), and for the other shed they are lifted up by hand (Figure 2–10c) so that they cross the threads *in the* heddles, which are *always stationary*. For either shed, insert the hand between the upper and lower parts of the warp behind the heddles and push the "O" threads up or down. The weft is woven in on a small shuttle which acts as beater at the same time.

2–9. Three belts woven on small looms. *From left to right:* inkle belt by Stana Coleman; cardwoven belt by Georgia Suiter; and inkle belt by a student.

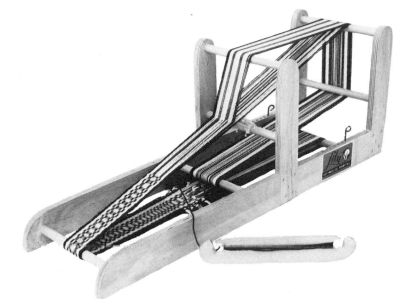

2–10. Inkle loom showing shuttle, which is also used as a beater, and partly woven warp. Photo courtesy of Lily Mills Company.

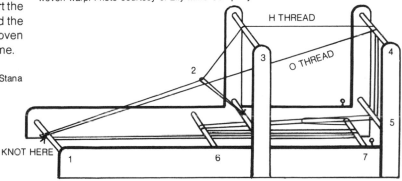

2–10a. Inkle loom, showing correct threading of two warp ends.

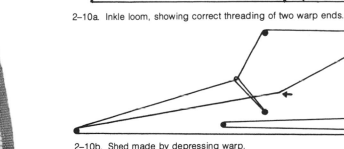

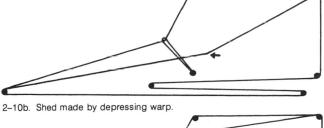

2–10b. Shed made by depressing warp.

2–10c. Shed made by raising warp.

Warp-faced stripes and many pick-up designs can be made on this efficient simple loom. Books dealing in detail with inkle weaving give many variations, suggestions, and specific instructions. Only one of many types of inkle looms is illustrated here. The examples of band weaving in Figures 2–11 and 2–11a and the explanations in this section should act as an incentive for further exploration of these band-weaving techniques. Even the most experienced weaver is enriched by mastering a new tool with which to express his ideas.

2–11a. Finger-weaving is a simple non-loom technique that requires tension on only one end of the warp. Shown here is a variation based on braiding methods of the Osage Indians.

COLLARS AND JEWELRY (COILING AND PIN WEAVING)

A completely different and imaginative aspect of weaving opened up when weavers started to create woven collars and jewelry, such as the *Chinese Ceremonial Neckpiece* shown in Figure 2–12. The inspiration for this came from three paintings of Chinese origin which the weaver saw at an exhibition. All the work was done on the loom, using silk, beads, and collected treasures, This adornment can be woven with a full-length back, as a tunic, or, as shown here, with a halter neck.

The pendant in Figure 2–13 was made without the use of a loom. In a technique related to macramé and tatting, it was made by wrapping half-hitch knots (Figure 2–13a) of orange wool around a core of heavy wool or jute. The addition of small Peruvian bone disks, tassels, knotted fringes, and a braided-wool chain makes an attractive necklace that could easily double as a wall decoration.

2–11. Two belts by Stana Coleman. *Above:* belt in a four-harness pattern weave; *below:* finger-woven belt.

2–12. *Chinese Ceremonial Neckpiece* by Marjorie Thurman; photo courtesy of the artist.

2–13. Knotted necklace in orange wool with bone disks, by Stana Coleman; photo by John W. Rosenthal.

2–13a. Half-hitch knot.

Coiling

Two charming and inventive necklaces were made in yet another technique, namely coiling This is a basketry technique in which a yarn is evenly wrapped around a heavy core. A tapestry needle is used to fasten each coil to the one below in a figure-eight or other basketry stitch (see Figure 2–15a, no. 5). In both pieces tiny beads were worked in as an understated decoration. The snail (Figure 2–15) is wrapped with linen, the other pendant (Figure 2–14) is wrapped with wool. Varying the fineness of the wrapping and the thickness of the core make differences in the total effect. Many materials can be used, but one must be sure that the core is as stiff or as pliant as necessary for the purpose planned. Directions for the technique of coiling (Figure 2–15a) are as follows (kindly supplied by Kathy Malec):

2–15. Snail necklace in coiling technique by Sherry Boemmel; collection of the author.

2–14. Coiled necklace by Susan Feulner; collection of the author.

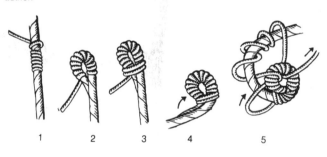

2–15a. Coiling technique; diagram by Kathy Malec.

(1) Cut end of core material (jute) into a wedge shape. With wrapping material, wrap tightly toward cut end for approximately 1 inch, folding the end inside.

(2) Bend the wrapped end to form a small circle.

(3) Wrap twice to secure circle.

(4) Squeeze core material around wrapped circle to make it round.

(5) Wrap two to four more times, then with a tapestry needle sew the wrapping yarn through the hole of the circle in figure-eight fashion. Continue wrapping the core several times, then use the figure-eight stitch to fasten each row to the preceding one.

Shapes can be made by keeping the coils flat or by sewing them gradually on top of each other. Another stitch, the lace or mariposa stitch is illustrated in Chapter 5 (Figure 5–15a). Other methods of basket-making may be found in the small, informative book *Basketry* by F. J. Christopher (see References).

Pin weaving

Pin weaving is especially suited for making versatile collars, which, like belts, give an individual touch to basic dresses and reflect the skill and creativity of the weaver. The collar shown in color on page 51 (Figure C–7), is pin weaving in which the warp and weft themselves form the shape, with wrapping and beads included.

Pin weaving can be done on cardboard or fiberboard, with pins forming the inner and outer outlines of the collar (Figure 2–16). A single thread is drawn back and forth around the pins to form the warp. The weft is then woven around and through this with a blunt needle. Note that the inner edge of the collar has to be closely woven in order to give the necessary support, and that an opening must be planned for the front or back to provide a way of wearing the collar. The opening can be fastened with button and loop, or long ends may be left to be braided for a bow tie. The weave itself can include tapestry, plain weave, wrapping, or any other technique the weaver may wish to apply.

2–17. Heidi Roberts demonstrates the correct set-up and position for cardweaving; photo courtesy of Irene A. Sherwin.

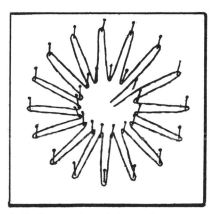

2–16. The technique of pin weaving.

CARDWEAVING

Cardweaving, or, as it is sometimes called, tablet weaving, is as captivating and interesting as a weaver's enthusiasm can make it. The cardwoven skirts, belts, and trimmings (see Figure 2–9 and Figures C–3 and C–5 on page 50) and the necklaces illustrated in Figure 2–18 are a few of the contemporary applications which are possible with this technique. The method is said to have originated in ancient Egypt and has been used continuously in many parts of the world since early historic times. Sometimes cardweaving seems difficult to handle, but the directions given below (kindly supplied by Irene A. Sherwin) are clear and easy to follow, so that even a child can do cardweaving. An enormous range of designs can be created by cleverly manipulating the threading and turning of the cards.

2–18. Cardwoven choker and necklace by Irene A. Sherwin.

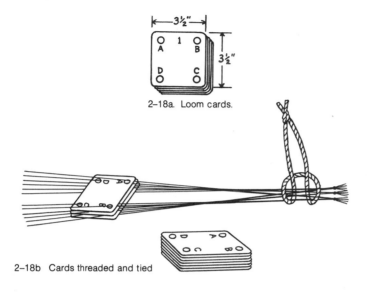

2–18a. Loom cards.

2–18b Cards threaded and tied

2–18c. Draft for ten-card design. *From bottom:* design on graph paper; threading sequence of individual cards; and cards threaded in direction of arrows in draft.

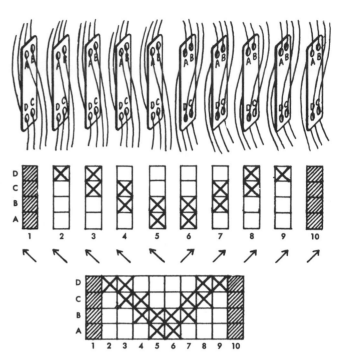

The loom cards

The loom cards are made from sturdy but lightweight cardboard which is shaped and hole-punched (Figure 2–18a). Each card should be 3½ inches square and rounded at the corners, with holes punched about 1 inch in on the diagonal from each corner. Label these holes A, B, C, D in clockwise direction as shown. The holes work similarly to the harnesses on a four-harness loom.

For this sample use 10 cards. Number each card consecutively in the center of the card. The number of cards relates to the width of the piece to be woven, as the diagram shows (Figure 2–18c). The more cards there are, the more warp ends there will be.

The design

The design is based on warp color arrangements. On graph paper mark off along the horizontal line a number of squares equal to the number of cards you are using—10 in this sample. Along the vertical line mark off 4 squares; these correspond to holes A, B, C, and D. This sample shows a pattern which has a single row of one color along each border and an arrow design in a second color against a third background color.

The warp

Each one of the 10 cards will be threaded according to what is indicated in the four "harness" squares below the number on the graph which corresponds to the number in the center of the card. Card 1 will be threaded with one end of the border color through each hole; card 2 will have one end of the background

color through each of holes A, B, and C, and an end of the arrow color through hole D, and so on.

Since each square represents one thread, you can count the number of threads to be cut of each color by counting the number of squares showing that color. This sample uses 8 threads of the border color, 18 of the background color, and 14 for the arrow. Cut the necessary number of threads to the correct length for your project, plus about 2 feet. This sample could be made for a headband using warps of about 40 inches in length.

Threading the cards

The cards may be threaded from the back to the front (the side with the letters) or from front to back. Threading the card from the front or back changes the direction of the warp twist which is the characteristic of card weaving, and therefore affects the design. The arrows drawn along the bottom of the graph will indicate the direction of the threading; in this case the first five cards are threaded from front to back, and the cards numbered 6 to 10 from back to front.

Place the warp threads on a table. Using the graph as a guide, thread 4 ends of the appropriate colors in the direction indicated for each card, pulling the threads for about 10 inches through the holes, and knot the four ends together (Figure 2–18b). Stack the cards face up with the letters all in the same order, with card 10 on top, and extend the knotted ends straight out in one direction and the long ends in the other direction to prevent tangling. When the cards are threaded, secure them in a pack with a rubber band. Tie the 10 knots together firmly by making a loop knot in one end of an 8-inch loop of strong cord, as shown in the diagram. Attach the open end of the loop to a rigid hook, such as a doorknob. It is best, however, to select the height of this rigid support according to the weaver's preference. A height of 5 or 6 feet from the ground provides a most satisfactory angle. Hold the pack of cards, still held together with the rubber band, sideways. With the fingers of the other hand or a large-toothed comb, straighten the long ends of the unknotted warp until all threads are smooth and in good order. Gather all threads in one hand and apply some tension. With the other hand slide the cards gently down the warp, as it is straightened, checking and smoothing until a clear natural shed appears from the cards to the ends. Keep the pack of cards about 12 inches from the unknotted end. Finally, tie a single knot with the ends of the upper shed and a single knot with the ends of the lower shed, near the end of the warp.

Setting up the backstrap

At this point, the weaver has the option of attaching the weaving end of the warp also to a stationary object or choosing a backstrap for tension. In this example the backstrap system is used, so that tension will be controlled by attaching the warp ends to a belt or cord which wraps around the weaver's waist.

Make this backstrap from the same kind of strong cord as used for the other loop. Measure it about 8 or 9 feet long and double it by knotting the ends together to form a loop. Attach this loop just above the 2 warp knots.

Pass the doubled cord around the weaver below the waist for maximum comfort. Fasten the other end of the cord back at the same place to make the backstrap. The weaver should sit in a comfortable straight chair at a distance that will draw the warp ends straight and taut but not too tight.

Remove the rubber band from the card pack by sliding it down the warp to your waist. This way it will be available again to secure the pack of cards when you wish to get up while the weaving is still unfinished.

Weaving

Start to weave for the first 8 turns with a heavier weft to spread the warp. This weft can be removed when the weaving is completed. Use a weft of the same color as the warp in cards number 1 and 10. Wind the weft thread into a butterfly or use it on a small shuttle. Do not have it too long since it is easy to lay in a new one at any time: put the new end along the old end, and weave them simultaneously for one or two rows. Cut off the tags later.

(1) Starting with the cards in A-D position (holes A and D are on top) and with the front of the cards (lettered sides) to the weaver's right (Figure 2–18d), pass the weft through the natural shed made by the A and D warp threads on top and the B and C warp threads below.

(2) Holding the cards loosely in both hands, rotate the tops of the cards *toward* the weaver, so that the A and B holes now are on top. Pass the weft through this new shed (turning in the beginning end of the weft yarn as in ordinary weaving) and beat it close to the first weft, using your fingers, shuttle or the long edge of a ruler.

(3) Rotate the cards again toward the weaver, so that now B and C holes are on top. Pull snugly on the weft in the previous shed to make the selvage even, then pass it through the new shed and beat back.

(4) Rotate the cards again toward the weaver so that the C and D holes are on top and weave as before.

(5) Turn the cards one more time toward the weaver, to the A-D position. Weave and beat the weft in as before. At this point the design of the draft can be identified in the small woven piece.

The design can be reversed in the weaving if the cards are now turned 4 times *away* from the weaver and the weft is inserted after each turn, as follows:

(1) A-D to D-C
(2) D-C to B-C
(3) B-C to A-B
(4) A-B to A-D

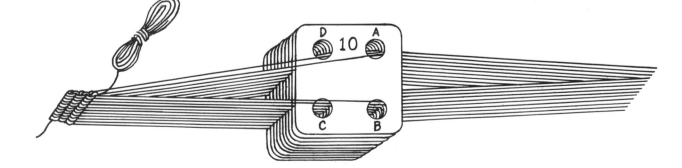

2–18d. Cards in the upright position, ready for weaving.

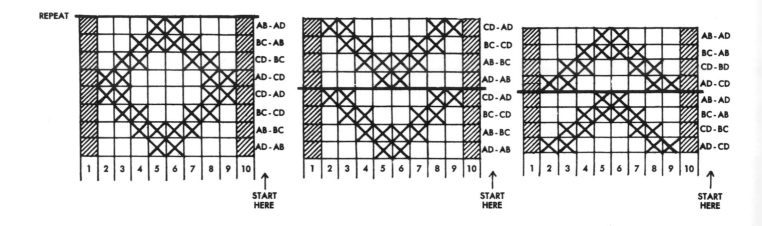

Left chart rows (top to bottom): AB-AD, BC-AB, CD-BC, AD-CD, CD-AD, BC-CD, AB-BC, AD-AB

Middle chart rows (top to bottom): CD-AD, BC-CD, AB-BC, AD-AB, CD-AD, BC-CD, AB-BC, AD-AB

Right chart rows (top to bottom): AB-AD, BC-AB, CD-BD, AD-CD, AB-AD, BC-AB, CD-BC, AD-CD

Columns for all: 1 2 3 4 5 6 7 8 9 10

START HERE (under each chart)

2–18e. Drafts for weaving variations. *From left:* turning cards four turns toward the weaver, four turns away from the weaver; turning cards continuously toward weaver; turning cards continuously away from the weaver.

Variations

A little practice and observation of various color arrangements and the results in turning the cards toward you or away from you in different rotations will increase understanding in a short time and provide ideas for creative designs.

Possibilities for variations are many. Part of the stack of cards may be turned in one direction, and another part turned in the other direction before inserting the weft. The cards may be divided and each section woven with a separate weft to form buttonholes or long slits. Cards may be moved to different positions to vary the color patterns of the design. New cards may be inserted with the new warp ends used as decorative tassels or woven into the weft. Cards may be removed and not woven for a space to make interesting floats. Cards may be turned a number of times without using any weft, employing the basic warp twining that makes cardweaving unique.

Cards of a different number of sides may be used, such as hexagonal cards with six holes, triangular cards with three holes, etc. A hole may be made in the center of each card to carry a heavy thread for added strength.

If the weft is passed from the same side each time and if the weft floats on the back are drawn up tightly after a few inches have been woven, a rope or closed tube will be formed.

Double-layered weaves may be made by using A and B warps for one layer and the C and D warps for the other, and then weaving the top and bottom layer each with a separate weft. Double-width or tubular weaves may be made using one weft. This produces a fabric that is a regular weave rather than a twined structure.

The weaving may be made wider and narrower by varying the tension of the weft on the edges. When the weft is not drawn tightly, it will begin to show through the warp, producing another design variation. Weft may be extended beyond the edge to make picots or, if extended farther, to make a fringe. All the possibilities are challenging to the creative weaver, and it is not surprising that there is a growing interest in this ancient method of weaving. Books dealing exclusively with cardweaving are listed in the Bibliography.

METAL AND FIBER COMBINATIONS

Crafts are no longer divided into separate areas, as they were in former times, by the material used. Metal and fiber combinations can produce exciting results, especially when the weaving or other textile technique is done directly with wire instead of yarn. Metalwork itself is no longer confined to gold and silver, for a piece does not have to be precious to be appreciated for the beauty of its design and craftsmanship.

The circular copper neckpiece in Figure 2–19 is woven on a 10-inch-square plywood board, with finishing nails placed around it in a circle. A hole is cut in the middle of the board, with a diameter of 6 inches, so that the technique of spool weaving can be employed. Instead of yarn, a fine-gauge wire is used. The drawing (Figure 2–19a) illustrates the fashion in which the wire is placed around the nails in a counterclockwise direction, leaving a tail of 8 inches at the beginning. Only the first row of looping is shown in the diagram. The interlocking rows are made as follows (directions kindly supplied by Pattie Frazer):

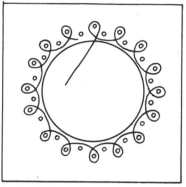

2-19. Circular copper necklace by Pattie Frazer; photo courtesy of the artist.

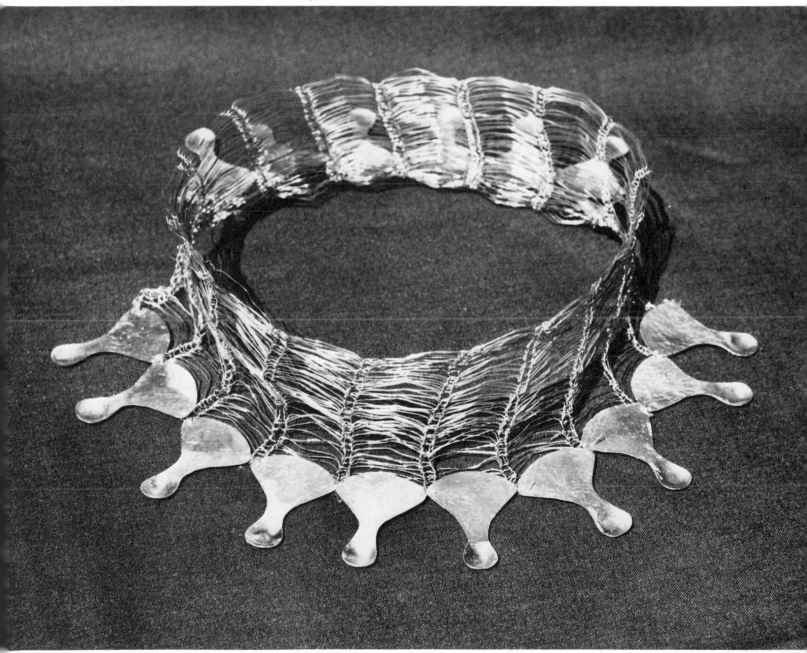

Carry the wire across the front of the nail above the loop below. With a crochet hook pick up the loop below and slip it over the top piece of wire, until it drops off the nail. Continue in this way around the circle for the desired number of rows. Pass the wire over the outside nails only. The inner nails are there only to make the looping over the outside nails easier. Normally stitches would be cast off to end the project, but in this neckpiece the shaped copper pieces, cut from a thin sheet of copper and pounded for texture, are attached to the last loops with copper-colored thread. This technique has many possibilities, not only for wire, but also for fiber constructions.

The linked silver necklace in Figure 2–20 also combines weaving with metal. Here die-formed squares of sterling silver backed with brass act as looms. Tiny holes are punched and strung with fine silver wire for the warp. The weft is silk buttonhole thread. Each piece is woven with a needle in different designs and colors. When the weaving is completed, the two halves of each square are riveted together.

Two artists, one a weaver, one a metal craftsman, collaborated to create a series of outstanding brooches, some of which, shown in Figures 2–21 and 2–22, are combination pieces of gold, silver, ivory, and metallic gold threads. The weaving is extremely delicate, and the designs form a perfect unity out of ordinarily unrelated media. See Chapter 6 for additional work resulting from this collaboration.

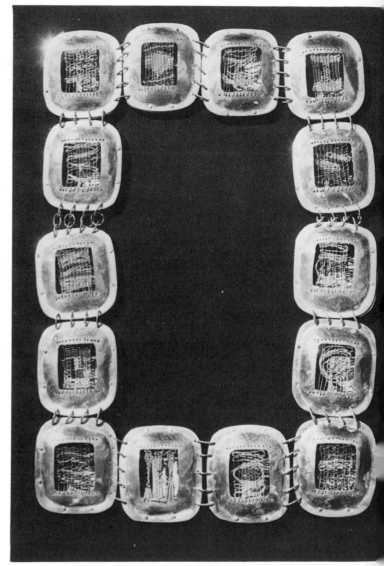

2–20. Silver necklace with woven centers, by Pattie Frazer; photo courtesy of the artist.

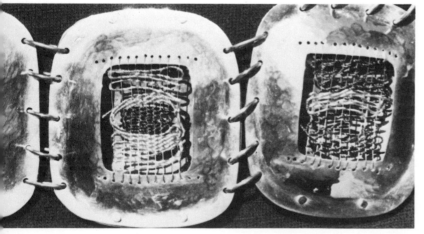

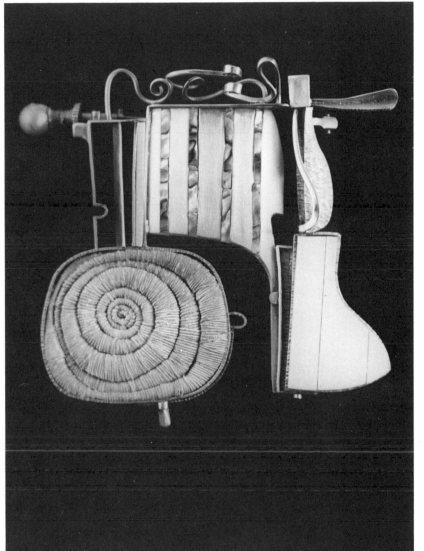

2–21. Combination metal and fiber brooch, 4 x 4 inches, by metalsmith Richard Mafong and weaver Jon Riis; photo courtesy of the artists.

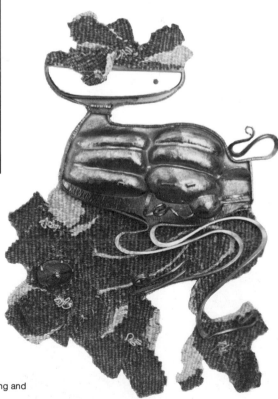

2–22. Combination silver and fiber brooch, 4 x 7 inches, by Richard Mafong and Jon Riis; photo courtesy of the artists.

3 FABRICS FOR INTERIORS

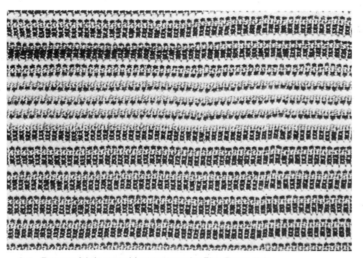

3-1. Drapery fabric on gold rayon warp by Else Regensteiner.

3-2. Black and gold upholstery fabric in wool and metallic threads on rayon warp by Else Regensteiner.

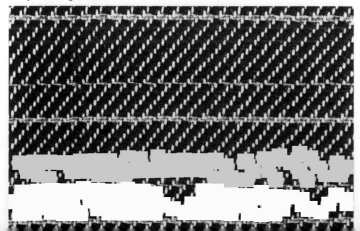

As clothing is the surrounding for the body, so interior furnishings are the clothing that surrounds our way of life. Fabrics for interiors are an expression of our taste and ability to combine function with art, when they are individually woven rather than being mass produced.

These fabrics can be combined in a coordinated interior design so that upholstery, drapery, pillows, and rugs harmonize or contrast excitingly with each other. Pillows have gained new importance as accents in a room, and handwoven rugs are frequently works of art as well as functional floor coverings.

UPHOLSTERY

There are fads and fashions in weaving and, in many instances, the main object is decoration. Upholstery's primary purpose, however, is functional, although it does have decorative importance. This is made very clear to the weaver when an upholsterer, upon starting work, takes a precious piece of fabric by diagonal corners and pulls it as hard as he can to test its strength. Strength is important because upholstery has to submit to abrasion, and the criterion for its usability is based not on the beauty of the weave, the sparkle of the colors, or the richness of the textures but on the result of merciless rubbing.

The environment in which interior fabrics will be used must also be considered. Exposure to strong sunlight; possible proximity to a bathing area, in which case people might come in wearing wet bathing suits; extremes of heat and coldness in the climate; and intended use (to decide whether the surface should be smooth or rough) all must determine the selection of fibers, weave, texture, and color.

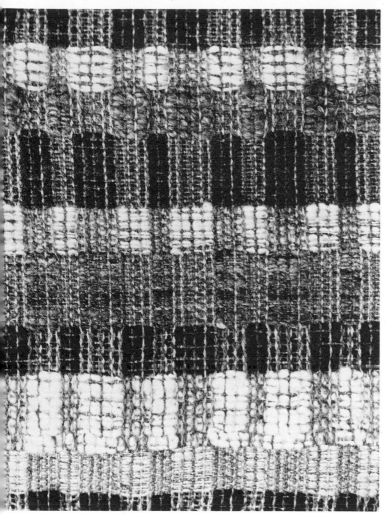

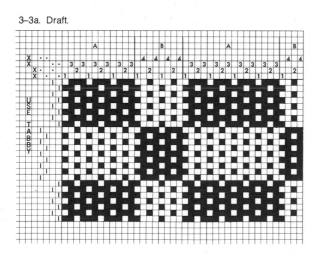

3–3. Upholstery fabric in Summer and Winter pattern, woven of handspun yarns from 29 different sheep, by Joyce Miller.

In commercial fabrics many synthetic fibers are used; the handweaver, in most cases, prefers natural fibers such as cotton, wool, mohair, linen, or silk because they seem to be more congenial to handweaving and more satisfying to the touch. In Figure 3–3 the upholstery fabric, in Summer and Winter pattern, is made of wool the handweaver spun herself, in natural shades from 29 different sheep.

3–3a. Draft.

Designing upholstery fabric

Warp threads for upholstery must be strong and sleyed close enough to make the fabric homogeneous in warp and weft. Of course the sleying varies according to the size and weight of the warp threads and the texture and thickness of the weft. As in clothing material, a sample made in several sleyings side by side will be a great help in designing the fabric which best fulfills all requirements of its intended function. One must remember, though, that a narrow sample will beat down much closer than a wider piece. It is important, therefore, in upholstery, to make a sample which approximates the actual width of the final material.

3–4. Plaid upholstery fabric in greens and golds woven with silk and wool yarns by Else Regensteiner and Julia McVicker.

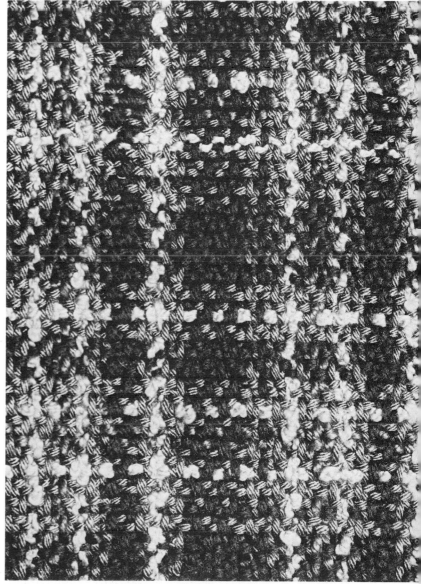

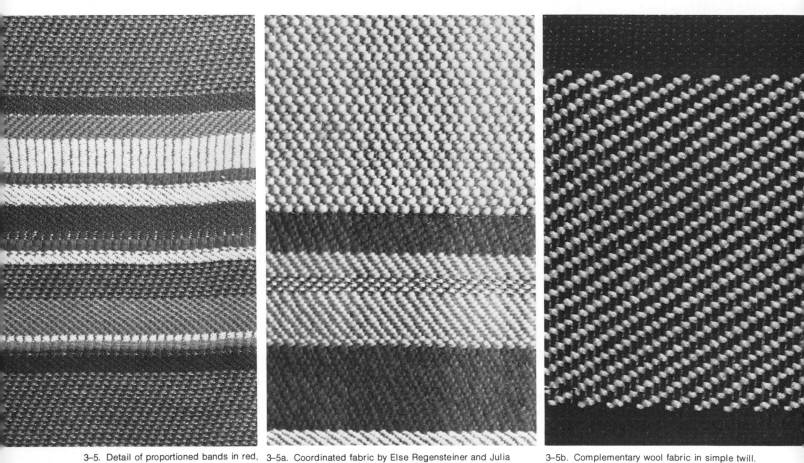

3–5. Detail of proportioned bands in red, black, tan, and copper upholstery fabric by Else Regensteiner and Julia McVicker.

3–5a. Coordinated fabric by Else Regensteiner and Julia McVicker.

3–5b. Complementary wool fabric in simple twill.

Concerning threadings, upholstery can be made in any weave avoiding long skips on the surface that would catch or be easily worn by abrasion. Twills and herringbones, block patterns, double weaves, and sometimes Beiderwand (a double-faced fabric of compound structure which originated in 18th century Germany) make the most interesting and successful upholstery fabrics. The three coordinated upholstery fabrics shown here (Figures 3–5, 3–5a, 3–5b) are made on the same warp of a strong sea-island cotton twine threaded in twill on four harnesses. In Figure 3–5 twills in various directions, together with basketweaves and changes of color, make a large repeat of great interest. In a fabric like this, the proportions of each unit of design to the other units, as well as the overall size of the repeat

must be carefully considered. The textures in this fabric are mixed, as it uses wool, cotton, and metallic copper thread.

Any time a thin metal thread is used in an upholstery fabric, it should be supported in the same shed by another yarn so that the weave is undisturbed in case of breakage. It is also a good idea to protect the thread from the ever-present danger of abrasion by placing it between two heavier yarns.

Fabrics in a large repeat design of stripes or bold patterns can be successfully coordinated with all-over twills. For example, one fabric, the boldest pattern, could be used on a couch and the other on chairs in the same room. Figure 3–5b shows a simple twill to complement the twills and basketweaves of the coordinated fabrics.

Variations of twills are shown here in three fabrics woven on eight harnesses in one undulating twill threading (Figure 3–6, 3–7, and 3–8). These fabrics were woven on a black cotton warp in natural and white wools; although somewhat restless patterns, they are striking fabrics for a room, easily coordinated with plain-weave draperies in which the emphasis is mainly on interesting texture (Figure 3–9).

3–7. Upholstery fabric in undulating reversed twill design by Stana Coleman.

3–7a. Draft for 4/4 undulating twill on 8 harnesses.

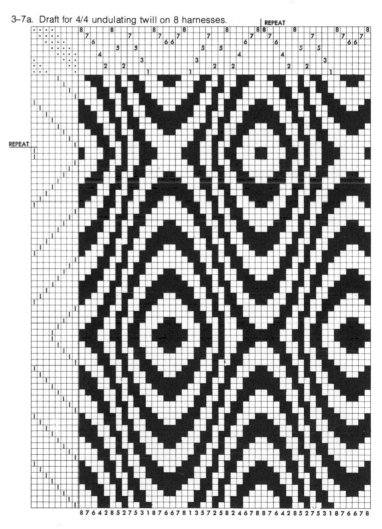

3–6. Upholstery fabric woven in undulating twill design on black warp with natural wool weft by Stana Coleman.

3–6a. Draft showing undulating 4/4 twill design.

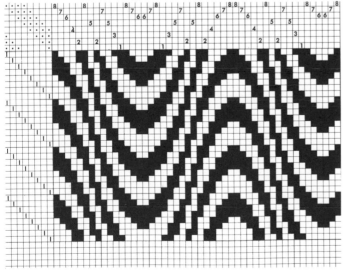

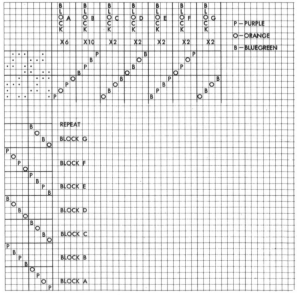

3–10. Double-weave fabric by Jane MacRae, also shown in color on page 74 (Figure C–21).

Double-weave upholstery

Double-weave upholstery can be designed in blocks or pattern weaves. Double weave is naturally a good choice for upholstery because the structural qualities of the double warp make it very sturdy.

Since, for drapery and upholstery, many yards of fabric are needed, the pattern must be loom controlled. This method works best when at least eight harnesses are used, so the heddles can be threaded in blocks of various colors and brought up in proportions according to the weaver's design. The sizes of the blocks must be determined before threading begins, but they can then be treadled as the weaver wishes, and designs can be developed through experimentation on the loom. Two colors are threaded alternately in the heddles on the first four harnesses for the width of one block, other colors are threaded alternately on the second four harnesses for the width of the next block.

3–10a. Draft. Note that the colors change in the blocks after the repeat.

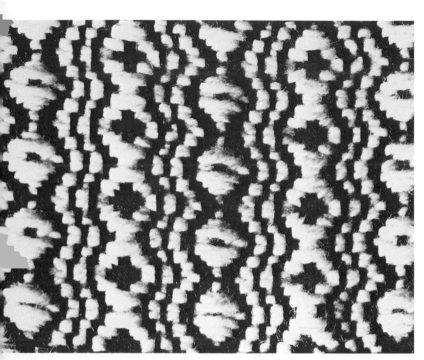

3–8. Upholstery fabric in treadling variation on same warp as Figures 3–6 and 3–7, by Stana Coleman.

3–9. Plain-weave textured drapery fabric to coordinate with upholsteries, by Else Regensteiner and Julia McVicker.

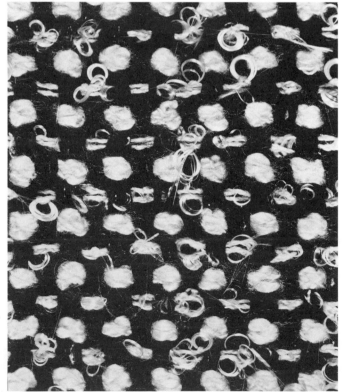

The play of colors as they are brought to the surface and disappear into the background, only to be replaced by others, can be fascinating and striking. In this upholstery fabric three colors were used: in the first block purple alternated with orange; in the second block blue alternated with purple; in the third block orange alternated with blue. If one changes the placement of the colors in the heddles after the third block, different colors are brought to the surface automatically across the width of the fabric, and six different blocks are achieved. The drafts show the threading of the colors in the heddles and the treadling sequence for this piece. The treadling sequence could be repeated enough times to make each color block square or could be changed to vary the length. A similar double-weave arrangement for a wall hanging is shown in color on page 75 (Figure C–25).

BEIDERWAND

An excellent weaving technique called Beiderwand, which handweavers have rarely explored for use in upholstery, drapery, or bedspreads, is found in some coverlets of German origin. Beiderwand is a double-faced rather than a double-layered construction. This means it is not a double weave, although it can be classified as a compound weave structure. To make this distinction clearer the weaver should recall that double weaves are compound structures because they have more than one set of warp and weft elements. We commonly understand that a double weave consists of two sets of warps which are woven on top of each other. If the double weave is tubular or is going to be opened out to make a double-width fabric then only one set of weft is used, but more commonly both warps are woven with

3–11. Coverlet in Beiderwand weave, by William A. Davis, 1918, Illinois. Woven to commemorate the end of World War I; photo courtesy of the Art Institute of Chicago

their own wefts, so that there are two sets of weft. Their surfaces can be interchanged and are therefore connected at the edges of the pattern.

Simple weaves, on the other hand, are composed of only one set each of warp and weft elements. There are many ways of making a simple weave into a compound weave by adding sets of elements to the simple weave structure, which then serves as the ground structure in the weaving. Examples are extra pattern threads as for brocading, floats, pile, etc., or extra warp threads as in supplementary warp structures (see page 59), which can be used decoratively or for added strength.

In *Coverlets, A Handbook on the Collection of Woven Coverlets in the Art Institute of Chicago,* Mildred Davison and Christa C. Mayer-Thurman describe Beiderwand as "The German term for a compound weaving structure which combines warp-faced plain weave with weft-faced plain weave. These two constructions reverse themselves throughout the fabric. Also characteristic are the vertically running ribs which are caused as a result of warp-thread groupings." These groups are divided by two different binding threads which are placed on specific harnesses.

The pattern is formed by floats of free weft threads held fast by the binding threads. Since every fifth thread only is a binder, these binder threads are placed on a second warp beam to assure evenness of tension. In some coverlets these binding threads are finer and of a different color than the threads of the ground warp. The fabric is reversible, and, because of the regularity of the weave, it is not always clear which side is meant to be the front.

Beiderwand is a block pattern that can be represented on a profile draft. However, it differs from the Summer and Winter system because in Beiderwand each pattern block requires two harnesses and two treadles, and the two front harnesses are reserved for the binding threads. Therefore a minimum of six harnesses is needed for a pattern with two blocks, eight harnesses for three blocks, etc. A tabby must be used between each pattern pick. The weft yarn for the pattern is thicker than that of background and tabby. Note that the tabby is not a "pure" plain weave in the regular 1/1 interlacing. but weaves with two threads at the points of interlacement with the binding threads.

Each treadling sequence can be repeated until a block of the desired size is formed. Blocks can be used singly or in combinations, as long as the alternating binding threads are raised with the block combinations, and alternating tabbies thrown between each pattern pick. Designs are limited by the number of harnesses, but arrangements of profile drafts give great scope for many interesting patterns.

As already explained, two warps are needed: the ground warp, which controls the pattern, and the binder warp. The binder warp should be one and a half times longer than the ground warp, because it has more take-up. This warp can also be used like a supplementary warp with skeins hanging weighted over the back beam (see Figure 3–16). On the sample shown in Figure 3–12 the binder warp has 5 threads per inch on one

3–12. Sample of Beiderwand weave in white cotton and red wool by Judith Gordon.

beam. The second beam has 20 ends per inch, and carries the pattern threads, and the total number of binder and pattern threads is 25 threads per inch. The pattern is controlled by the threads on the second beam.

    block 1 - threaded on harnesses 3 and 4
    block 2 - threaded on harnesses 5 and 6
    block 3 - threaded on harnesses 7 and 8

The reed was 10 dents per inch, sleyed alternately 4, 1, 4, 1 in the dents. General threading, tie-up and treadling sequences are shown in Figure 3–12 b And weaving sequence is as follows.

To weave block 1, treadle:

    A plus 1 is 1–3–4; use 1 pick wool
    Tabby Y is 4–6–8; use 1 pick cotton
    B plus 1 is 2–3–4; use 1 pick wool
    Tabby X is 3–5–7; use 1 pick cotton

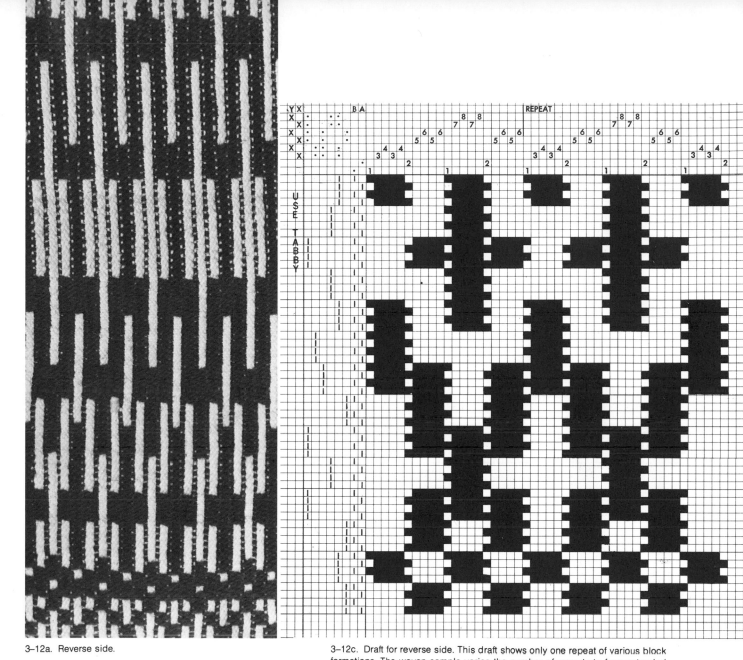

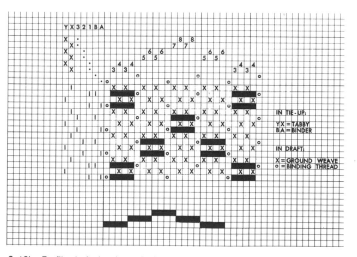

3–12a. Reverse side.

3–12c. Draft for reverse side. This draft shows only one repeat of various block formations. The woven sample varies the number of repeats to form extended blocks. The binder thread is shown in the design. The ground weave (tabby) is not shown. Use opposite tie-up for other side.

3–12b. Profile draft showing principle of weave.

IN TIE-UP:

YX = TABBY
BA = BINDER

IN DRAFT:

X = GROUND WEAVE
o = BINDING THREAD

To weave block 2, treadle:

    A plus 2 is 1–5–6; use 1 pick wool
    Tabby Y is 4–6–8; use 1 pick cotton
    B plus 2 is 2–5–6; use 1 pick wool
    Tabby X is 3–5–7; use 1 pick cotton

To weave block 3, treadle:

    A plus 3 is 1–7–8; use 1 pick wool
    Tabby Y is 4–6–8; use 1 pick cotton
    B plus 3 is 2–7–8; use 1 pick wool
    Tabby X is 3–5–7; use 1 pick cotton

The tie-up is reversed when the opposite side is desired as the surface or if a sinking shed (counter-balanced) loom is used. Figures 3–12 and 3–12a show a Beiderwand sample, designed and woven in the same warp setting described above, but using a different profile draft and different combinations of blocks in the treadlings.

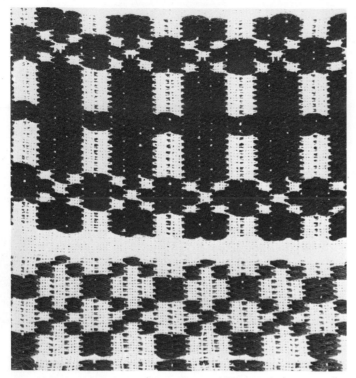

3–13. Beiderwand samples by Margaret Sheppard. Woven on the same warp, the top sample is black wool, the bottom sample is wine-colored stranded cotton.

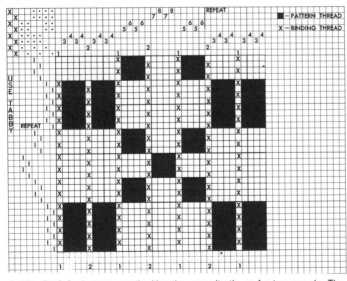

3–13a. Draft for bottom sample. Use the opposite tie-up for top sample. The tabby is not shown in the draft, and the weft is shown in black as used for the sinking shed.

The versatility and interest of this characteristic weave is shown in the two samples here. In Figure 3–13 the warp was 20/2 cotton in natural color, 30 threads per inch, sleyed double in each dent in a 15-dent reed. The top part of the weaving is treadled in a tie-up opposite to the bottom part. Beiderwand offers a fascinating challenge for exploration and possibilities for many diverse purposes.

Continued on page 57.

COLOR SECTION 1

C–1. Wool cape in satin weaves by Kathryn Wertenberger; photo by Morris Wertenberger, Pix Productions. See Figure 1–18.

C–2. Vest with rya knots by a student; photo by Else Regensteiner.
C–3. Overskirt in patterned bands of cardweaving and dark bands made on the inkle loom, by Stana Coleman.
C–4. Tagari bag in "embroidery weave," designed by Koula Tapta and woven at the American Farm School in Greece; photo by Garcia. See Figure 2–8.
C–4a. "Embroidery weave" on the loom; photo by Else Regensteiner.
C–5. Swedish rya wool belt in cardweaving, by Stana Coleman.
C–6. *Bird in Cage,* hanging by Ethel Kaplan; photo by Dr. Max Kaplan.

C–7. Collar in pin weaving by Ethel Kaplan.

C–8. Fish mobile, pin weaving on wood, by Ethel Kaplan; photo by Else Regensteiner.

C–9. *Cinderella Michigan,* outfit by Barbara De Peaux; photo courtesy of the artist.

C–10. *Two Loons and Summer and Winter,* skirt by Barbara De Peaux. Front of skirt is shown; also see Figure 1–19. Photo courtesy of the artist.

C–10a. Detail of tapestry weave in skirt.

C–10b. Detail from the back of the skirt.

C–11. Multicolored toy ball by Barbara De Peaux; photo courtesy of the artist. See Figure 5–16.

C–12. Party muff by Barbara De Peaux; photo courtesy of the artist. See Figure 2–7.

C–13. Tubular woven dolls by Marcella Boettcher and Elizabeth Quist (center); photo by John W. Rosenthal.

C–14. *Rosie,* life-sized doll with removable head, by Gwynne Lott; photo courtesy of the artist.

C–15. Tubular woven dolls in Peruvian style, by Rosemarie Last; photo by John W. Rosenthal. See Figure 5–1.

C–16. Six-pointed star mobile by Brunhilde Holzhauer. See Figure 5–22.

C–17. Official Ottawa Tartan by Jean Docton of Canada.

C–18. Floor pillow in pattern weave by Astra Kleinhofs-Strobel; collection of Stana Coleman.

C–2

C–3

C–4

C–5

C–4a

C–9 ←

C–10

C–10b

C–10a

C-11

C-12

C-16

C-17

C-18

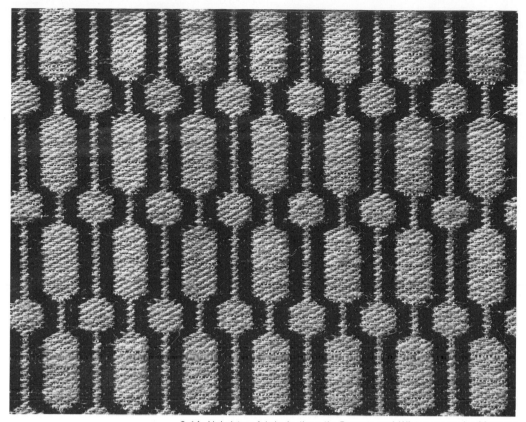

3–14. Upholstery fabric in three-tie Summer and Winter weave by Margaret Sheppard; photo courtesy of the artist.

UPHOLSTERY WEAVE VARIATIONS

The strong upholstery design in Figure 3–14 is adapted from a Finnish weave. The weaver developed the design from a Summer and Winter profile draft and was intrigued by achieving a twill effect in both patterns and background. Three harnesses are used for the tie-down threads instead of the usual two. The fabric is woven on opposite harness combinations with two shuttles, one for the pattern thread in one color, the other for the background thread in another color. The weight of both threads are the same. No tabby or binder is used, but one of the tie-down threads is always raised in steady rotation, together with one pattern pick (see Figure 3–14a). In this system, the tie-down threads, which are threaded on harnesses 1, 2, and 3 between the pattern threads, are always raised in regular twill rotation, and each tie-down thread is always raised together with a desired combination of pattern threads. The rotation of tie-down threads causes the fabric to have a twill effect in the pattern as well as in the background areas of the design.

This design is woven on a 20/2 natural cotton warp, set at 30 threads per inch, and woven with 7/1 linen for the pattern thread and black homespun wool for the background. The draft shows threading, tie-up, and treadling for this fabric. Since the background needs the first 3 harnesses, the pattern can only be threaded on the remaining harnesses. For two blocks five harnesses are necessary and for five blocks eight harnesses.

In the weft, the colors alternate in every pick. The rotation must stay the same, no matter what single block or block combinations are woven:

harness 1 plus pattern harnesses—color A
harness 1 plus opposite harnesses—color B
harness 2 plus pattern harnesses—color A
harness 2 plus opposite harnesses—color B
harness 3 plus pattern harnesses—color A
harness 3 plus opposite harnesses—color B

3–14a. Draft. The warp is light; the weft is alternately light and dark. The twill binder threads are not shown.

57

3–15. Drapery fabric in black-and-white color-and-weave effect by Takeko Nomiya.

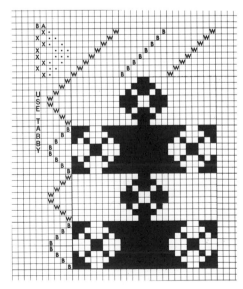

3–15a. Draft. Tabbies and interlacements in the solid white and solid black areas are not shown.

DRAPERY

Drapery materials are lighter weight and more supple than upholstery. These fabrics too must be designed with the proposed environment in mind. They may have to be sun-resistant and opaque or sheer and transparent. They must be flexible enough to drape, and woven closely enough not to sag. Draperies are often coordinated with upholstery (see Figures 3–1 and 3–2).

Figure 3–15 shows a drapery material made in a pattern achieved by combination of color and weave on eight harnesses. This fabric can be made of wool or cotton approximately the size of perle cotton #3. A fine tabby is used between the pattern picks to act as a binder.

DRAPERIES IN SUPPLEMENTARY WARP

A technique which is suitable and very interesting for drapery is the use of a supplementary warp. This is an extra warp, in a different color and heavier yarn, which is planned to make a pattern floating above or, where not needed, below the ground structure. The ground warp is threaded on the first two harnesses, while the supplementary warp is on the other harnesses. It can be used in several ways.

If a loom with only three harnesses is used, the supplementary warp can be put on harness 3 for a method in which the pattern is picked up with a stick.

Or, if four or more harnesses are used, the supplementary warp can be threaded in groups such as blocks or pattern threadings. Between each of the supplementary warp threads, one or two ground warps have to be threaded. If the ground warp is finer, as it usually is, then two warps should go between each supplementary warp and be threaded alternately on harnesses 1 and 2. If the ground warp and supplementary warps are the same thickness, only one warp is needed between the supplementary warps. The ground warp (or warps) and the single supplementary warp threads are then sleyed together in a single dent.

Since the tension of the two warps will be different, each should be wound separately on a different warp beam. If only one beam is available, the supplementary warp can hang in warp chains over the back beam, as shown in Figure 3–16. Tension for these chains is supplied by weights such as bottles, fishing weights, or even unopened soup cans. A wooden rod such as a broomstick can be slipped under the supplementary warp and held above the ground warp by two wooden blocks that can be easily made to sit on the back beam. When the supplementary warp is threaded in blocks, it facilitates the weaving if each block is put on a separate tension weight. Pick-up and loom-controlled methods for supplementary warps are described in the following sections.

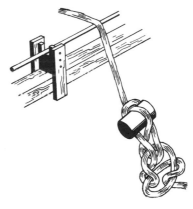

3–16a. Detail of rod on back beam.

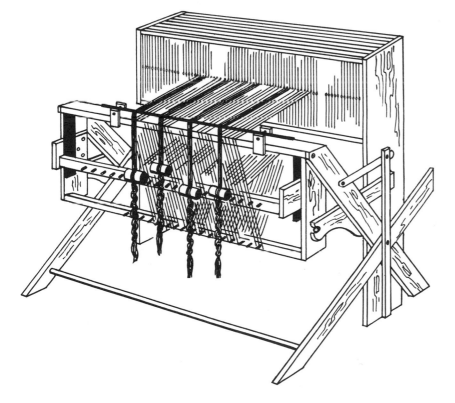

3–16. Loom with supplementary warp hanging over back beam.

3–16b. Detail of slip knot for weights and warp ends.

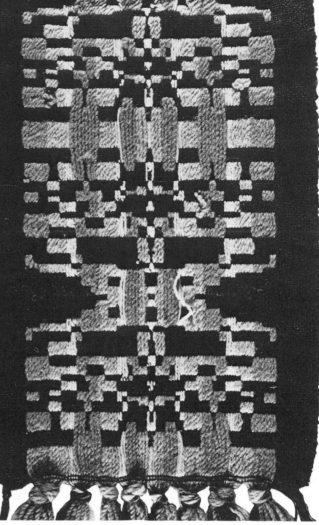

3–17. Supplementary warp pick-up design in bright colors on black background, made by a student; photo by Edward Miller.

3–17a. Reverse side.

Pick-up method
The threading is:

harnesses 1 and 2—ground warps

harness 3 (or harnesses 3 and 4)—supplementary warp

The weaving procedure is as follows:

(1) Treadle harness 1 and 2 alternately for border and weave.

(2) Raise harness 3. Pick up the pattern with pick-up stick.

(3) Drop harness 3, but *leave stick in the warp.*

(4) Raise harness 1 and weave.

(5) Raise harness 2 and weave.

(6) Continue this treadling for as long as desired. When changing the design, take out the stick and tie down by raising harness 1, weave, then raise harness 2.

(7) Repeat pick-up according to design.

In places where the pattern does not appear on the surface, the supplementary warp will float on the back. When the supplementary warp is threaded on harnesses 3 and 4, one or both harnesses can be raised for the pick-up pattern.

Loom-controlled method, four harnesses
Plan the design on graph paper in two blocks or small units.

The threading is:

harness 1—background thread (ground warp)

harness 2—background thread (ground warp)

harness 3—pattern thread for Block A (supplementary warp)

harness 4—pattern thread for Block B (supplementary warp)

The treadling is as follows:

plain background—1–2 alternately

block A—1–3

block A—2–3

block B—1–4

block B—2–4

To weave both blocks together, treadle:

1–3–4

2–3–4

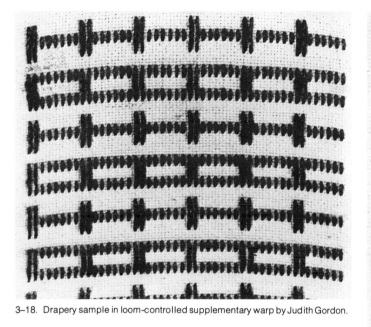

3–18. Drapery sample in loom-controlled supplementary warp by Judith Gordon.

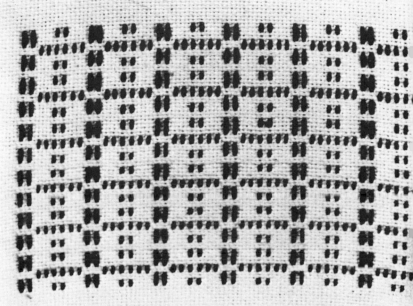

3–19. Variation on the same warp, by Judith Gordon.

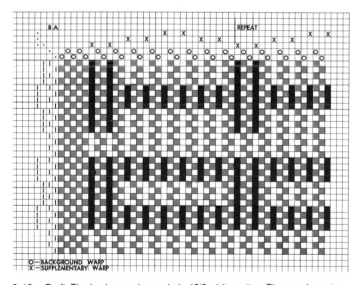

3–18a. Draft. The background warp is in 10/2 white cotton. The supplementary warp is 5/2 blue cotton. The 12 dent reed is sleyed with two white and one blue warp thread per dent.

3–19a. Reverse side.

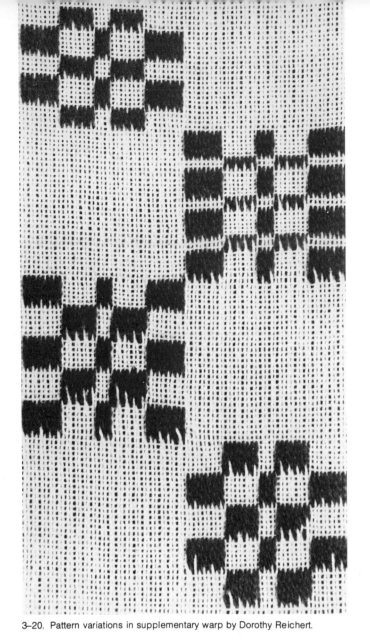

3–20. Pattern variations in supplementary warp by Dorothy Reichert.

The same principle, but with the background threads on harnesses 1 and 2 placed singly between the supplementary warp, is illustrated in Figure 3–20. Here six harnesses are used. The basic natural-colored mercerized cotton threads alternate with fine brown wool yarn in two different blocks. The supplementary warp is arranged for one block on harnesses 3 and 4 and for the other block on harnesses 5 and 6. As before, harnesses 1 and 2 are reserved for the ground warp, threaded 30 threads per inch in a 15-dent reed for the tabby areas, and 60 threads per inch with the supplementary warp in the pattern areas. Many threading and treadling variations give great scope for unusual designs, as the examples in this section illustrate.

Loom-controlled method, eight harnesses

On eight harnesses all but two harnesses can be pattern blocks. To get a better balance, the background threads can be distributed on harnesses 1 and 5. Any block can be raised together with one of the background threads, and blocks can be combined at will.

Long floats on the back have to be tied down once in a while with a plain weave or, when woven in well, can be cut off after weaving is finished and the piece removed from the loom.

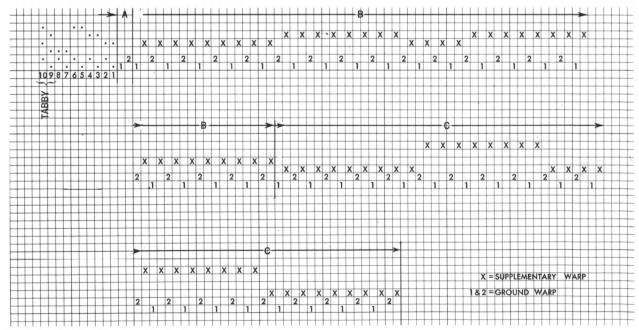

3–20a. Draft. Treadle 9 and 10 for tabby of combined pattern and ground (block A). For Block B, treadle 3 and 4 alternately to square; 1 and 2 alternately to square. For Block C, treadle 5 and 6 alternately to square; 7 and 8 alternately to square.

3–21. Detail of loom-controlled supplementary warp by Else Regensteiner.

3–22. Design in supplementary warp by Dee Nemeth.

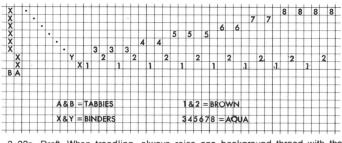

| A & B = TABBIES | 1 & 2 = BROWN |
| X & Y = BINDERS | 3 4 5 6 7 8 = AQUA |

3–22a. Draft. When treadling, always raise one background thread with the block combinations.

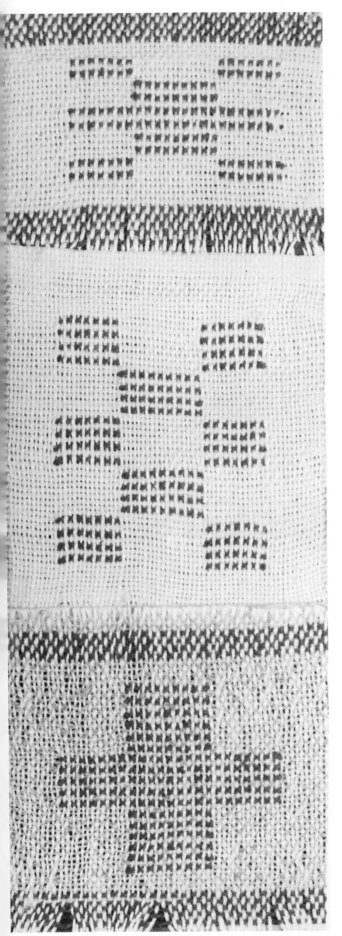

DRAPERIES IN SPOT WEAVE OR SWIVEL

The weave called *swivel* by American and Canadian weavers is actually not a swivel weave in the original meaning of the term. True swivel weave is made by a number of small shuttles laying in designs with extra weft on a ground or foundation cloth. Each swivel shuttle can have a different color and goes back and forth only over the area of its own small design. Raised spot designs, such as in dotted Swiss, are characteristics of this weave, which is commonly made on power looms with swivel attachments.

The name *swivel* as adopted by handweavers refers to a completely different method of weaving, by which a color appears in plain weave on the surface in brocade-like designs against a background of another color, while the back of the fabric has weft floats running from selvage to selvage. The weave is actually made by the loom-controlled use of color. For this method the design is basically arranged in blocks and can be treadled with many threadings, such as Summer and Winter, Crackle, or Rosepath. The blocks may be any length, but there must be a minimum of eight threads for a threading unit.

The method of weaving needs two weft threads, one similar or the same as the warp in color and weight, the other in a contrasting color. The pattern is made by three treadlings:

1 pattern pick (contrasting color)
1 background pick
1 tabby pick

This sequence of wefts is repeated for the length of one block, when the pattern pick changes according to the design.

The weave can start with any pattern pick. It is then followed by whichever background pick works with the pattern thread as a tabby. For example, for a sinking shed, if harness 4 is selected as the pattern pick, the background would be 2-4 and the tabby pick would be the opposite, 1-3. It is easiest to figure out the treadling for a sinking shed and convert it to the rising shed afterwards. Figures 3–23 and the draft show a simple two-block threading, for rising shed.

3–23. Three variations in spot weave (swivel weave) by Else Regensteiner.

3–23a. Draft. The tie-up is for the rising shed; pattern pick is indicated by a circle.

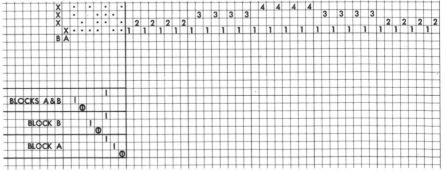

Threading:
    1, 2, 1, 2
    1, 3, 1, 3
    1, 4, 1, 4
    1, 3, 1, 3
    Repeat from start.
Tabby:
    1 and 2–3–4
Block A: 1–2–4 pattern
    1–3 background
    2–3–4 tabby
Block B: 1–2–3 pattern
    1–4 background
    2–3–4 tabby
Blocks A and B: 1–2 pattern
    1–3–4 background
    2–3–4 tabby

Other combinations of blocks can easily be found once a sample warp is threaded on the loom.

Both swivel and supplementary warp techniques can be used for upholstery as well as drapes. Figure 3–24 illustrates a green upholstery material in swivel weave using a warp of 2/16 mercerized cotton set 30 threads per inch in the reed. The weft is 2/8 onion-skin-dyed rayon for the pattern, but the same as the warp for the tabby and background picks. The floats of weft in back are not apparent on the surface.

3–24. Upholstery fabric in "swivel weave" by Jean Docton.

3–24a. Draft. The tie-up is for the rising shed.

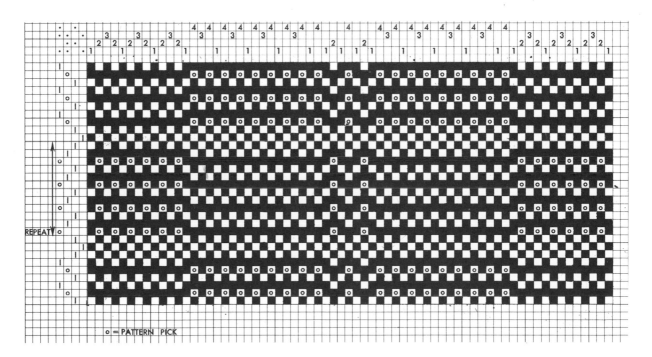

REPEAT

o = PATTERN PICK

65

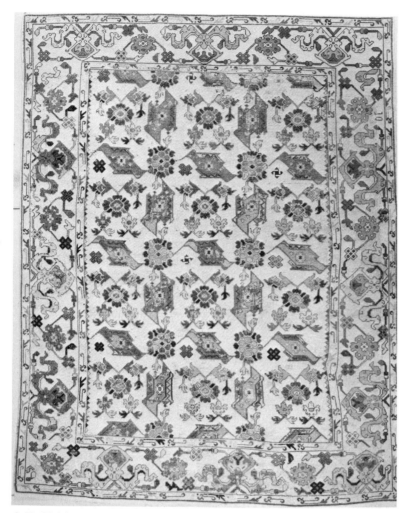

3–25. Bird design carpet from Western Anatolia, probably Ushak; photo courtesy of the Art Institute of Chicago; Gift of Joseph V. McMullan in memory of Margaret O. Gentles.

The age-old technique, however, was applied successfully to very different designs by a former missionary Mrs. Joice Loch. In 1928, she went with her husband to live in a large Byzantine tower in the village of Uranopolous at the frontier of Mt. Athos in northern Greece. The Greek government had taken over the land from the monastery and settled a small group of refugees from Asia Minor there. In order to help these people, some of whom were rug designers and weavers from Turkey, Mrs. Loch began to collect and adapt designs from Mount Athos.

The monastery at Mt. Athos still prohibits visits by women. In her book *Prosforion—Uranopolous, Rugs and Dyes*, Mrs. Loch wrote: "My husband, going to and from the monasteries, brought back photographs he had taken of Byzantine motifs, chiefly from illuminated parchments of books." She passed these designs along to the weavers and she also revived plant dyeing, insisting that the rugs be made in the authentic natural colors.

In Uranopolous (formerly called Pyrgos) and at the American Farm School in Thessaloniki these "Pyrgos" rugs are still being made in limited editions. They all carry the nutcracker eagle motif shown in Figure 3–26, which is the oldest form of the double-headed eagle on Mt. Athos. The symbol originates from the carved wooden nutcrackers which were used by the early hermits on the mountain.

3–26. Nutcracker eagle motif from Mount Athos. After drawing by Joice M. Loch.

RUGS

Rugs have been discussed exhaustively in many books, and most weavers are familiar with the various knots and methods of rug weaving. Therefore this section presents ideas for design and new applications of the ancient techniques.

Oriental rugs are known all over the world. The intricate designs of these rugs could not and should not be imitated by the contemporary weaver of the Western hemisphere, but the art is still alive in the Orient. The beautiful textures and glowing colors of the plant-dyed wools and silks cannot be surpassed

The rugs are woven on upright looms in Ghiordes knots, or what in Scandinavian countries is called the *flossa* technique. The warps are made of strong cotton, approximately 10/2 size, and set closely at 25 ends per inch. The pile consists of 25 knots per square centimeter and is knotted from a long thread which the weaver pulls down from balls of wool strung along the top of the loom. The wool thread is knotted into two warp threads with the left hand and then pulled down and cut with a small knife held in the weaver's right hand (Figure 3–27a). The fine plant-dyed wool is used in single strands. Knots of the same color are tied in each row wherever the design demands. Then the next color is filled in, until the row is completed. The design, drawn on graph paper, guides the weaver, who knots the design upside down.

3–27. *Pegasus,* pile rug from the American Farm School in Thessaloniki, Greece, collection of author; photo by John W. Rosenthal.

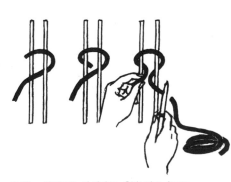

3–27a. Method of tieing Ghiordes knots with long strands of yarn cut with small knife.

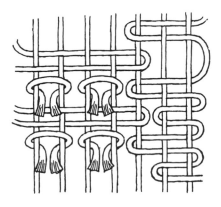

3–27b. Securing selvage with extra weft.

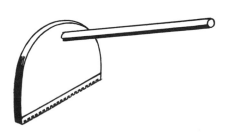

3–27c. Metal rug beater used in Greece.

Two cotton tabbies are used between each row of pile. The first tabby is laid in very loose arcs, then beaten down very tightly with a metal beater (Figure 3–27c). The second tabby is stretched straight across as a base for the next row of knots. The selvages are fortified with an extra cotton thread on each side which runs along the edges in a figure-eight weave. The pile, which is knotted 3 centimeters (1⅛ inches) high is clipped with curved scissors to a height of 1 centimeter (⅜ inch) after several rows of knots are woven. In a 32×42-inch rug there are 500,000 knots, and a girl can tie several thousand knots a day, depending on her skill and experience. The Pyrgos rugs shown here were made by Greek girls at the American Farm School.

3–28. *The Garden of Eden,* pile rug from the American Farm School in Thessaloniki, Greece, collection of author; photo by John W. Rosenthal.

3–28a. Detail.

3–28b. Girl weaving the rug; photo by Henry P. Williams III.

3–29. Owl rug, Greek design in closely knotted pile; photo by Stephanos Repellas.

3–29a. Zoetsa Mehaelidhou working on the rug. Note the balls of plant-dyed wools and the design on graph paper attached to the loom; photo by Stephanos Repellas.

69

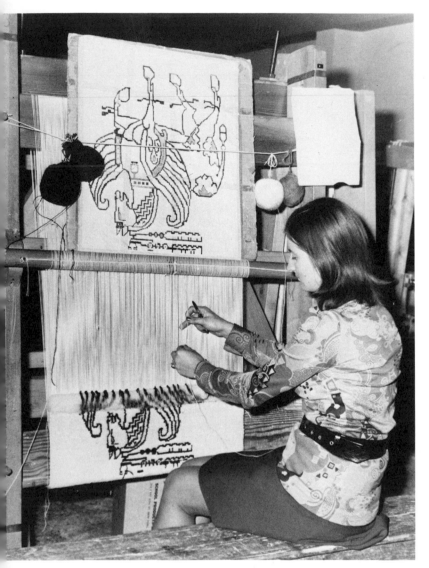

It is a never-ending surprise to discover the diverse creative ideas and the many different styles which can be produced by one and the same technique. Far removed from the design conception and the close pile of the Greek Pyrgos rugs are the rya carpets in Figures 3–31 and 3–32. Yet the knot is the same Ghiordes, or rya, knot (see Figure 3–33).

Long, shaggy piles, and free-running jagged lines of well-blended colors in earthy tones demonstrate a contemporary design approach in the rug in Figure 3–31. The wool is plied rya rug wool from Scandinavia, and the rows of knots are divided by many picks of tabby.

The ardent wish of craftsmen to use materials with utmost respect for their inherent qualities is realized in the rug shown in Figures 3–32 and 3–32a, which is made like a rya rug, with a linen warp set at 8 threads per inch, but knotted with unspun natural fleece at 4 knots per inch. The interesting feature of this rug is that the warp is threaded in a Rosepath pattern. Instead of the usual tabby, the backing is woven in handspun wools of various natural shades in a reverse twill treadling. The knotting in front shows faintly through the design on the back. Woven in this unusual method, the rug is completely reversible and could be used also as a warm blanket.

The bright geometric design in the rug shown in color on page 74 (Figure C–22) is very effective because of the dense pile in uneven length, made in Ghiordes-knot technique from Scottish and Persian wool yarns. A noticeable feature in this rug is the gradual reversal of the direction of the pile which makes the rug lie perfectly flat on the floor. The Ghiordes knot (Figure 3–33) is made upside down for about every third or fourth knot, beginning at the fifth row from the rug's end. This reversal of the pile is gradually continued up to the last two rows, where all the knots are made in reversed direction. No finishing is needed except for the several inches of flat plain weave, woven at the beginning and at the end of the rug, which are turned under and sewn.

3–30. Instructor Koula Taptá demonstrates tieing rug knots in the Pegasus rug. Note that the design is woven upside down; photo by Stephanos Repellas.

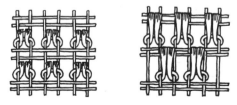

3–30a. Rug knots for short and long pile.

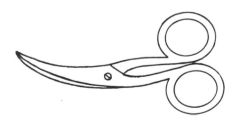

3–30b. Curved scissors for clipping pile.

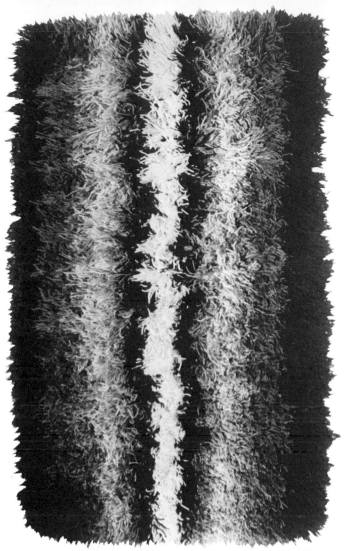

3–32a. Reverse side, showing Rosepath design.

3–31. Rya rug in long shaggy wool pile by Joyce Lopez; photo by Harold Nelson.

3–32. Rya rug woven from unspun and handspun wool by EuJane Taylor, collection of author.

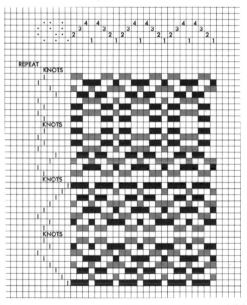

3–32b. Draft for reverse side. The weft is alternately dark and light.

3–33. Ghiordes or rya knot, as used in rug shown on page 74 (Figure C–22).

COLOR SECTION 2

C–19. Tubular weave pillow with stuffed pockets, by Mary Libby Neiman; photo by Michel Ditlove. See Figure 4–9.

C–20. Afghans and stoles in mohair and wool, by Mary Libby Neiman; photo by Michel Ditlove.

C–21. Double-weave fabric by Jane MacRae. See Figure 3–10.

C–22. Rya rug by Esther Gotthoffer; photo by Longley's Studio. See Figure 3–33.

C–23. Hanging in polychrome double weave by Georgia Suiter of New Zealand; photo courtesy of the artist.

C–24. Hanging in wrapped-warp technique, by Esther Gotthoffer; photo by Longley's Studio.

C–25. *Games,* combined double-weave and tapestry hanging by Astra Kleinhofs-Strobel. See Figure 6–39a.

C–26. *Funny Face,* small hanging in supplementary-warp technique, by Else Regensteiner; collection of Nancy C. Newman.

C–27. *Rectangles,* leno design on plain weave, 36 × 54 inches, by Else Regensteiner; photo by John W. Rosenthal.

C–28. *Red Feathers,* double-weave hanging by Else Regensteiner; photo by John W. Rosenthal; collection of the University of Houston.

C–29. *Design in Red and Blue,* hanging with open warp sections, by Else Regensteiner; photo by the artist.

C–30. Detail of hanging with tie-dyed warp and wrapped and woven weft by Fran Weintraub Lasky; photo courtesy of the artist.

C–31. Tapestry of woven bands by Jo Le Mieux; photo by Else Regensteiner.

C–32. *Woven Brocade,* hanging with tie-dyed cloth strips, by Cynthia Schira; photo courtesy of Marna Johnson.

C–33. *Bat,* tapestry by Joanna Staniszkis of Canada; photo courtesy of the artist.

C–34. *Hublot I,* tapestry by Monique Montandon of Switzerland; photo of Francois Martin.

C–35. *Firebird,* tapestry by Monique Montandon; photo by André Melchior.

C–36. *Spleen,* tapestry by Monique Montandon; photo by André Melchior.

C–37. *Sisters #2,* tapestry by Ruth Ginsberg-Place; photo courtesy of Marna Johnson.

C–38. *Circus Op,* hanging by Laurie Herrick; photo by Anne Dengler. See Figure 6–43.

C–39. *Burning Bush,* warp painting and weaving combination by Sharon Price; photo by Else Regensteiner.

C–40. *Mother and Child,* tapestry designed by Dr. Calvin Fisher and woven by Wendell H. Teegarden; photo by Else Regensteiner.

C–41. *The XI Moon,* wall plaque by Bettine Lawson; photo courtesy of the artist.

C-21

C-22

C–23

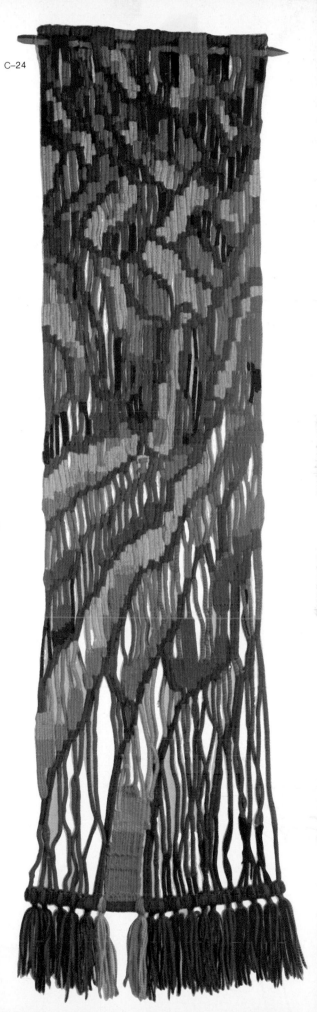

C–24

C–25

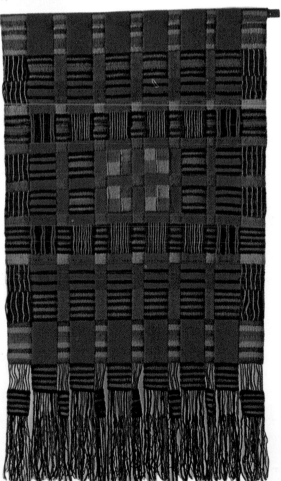

C-26

C-27

C-28

C-29

C–30

C–32

C–31

C–33

C–34

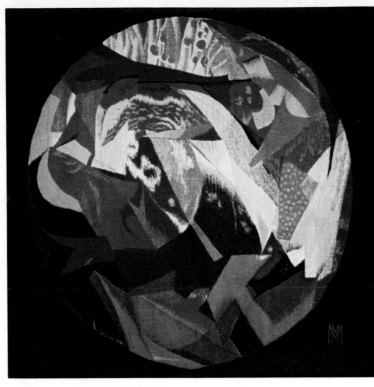

C–36

C–35

C–37

C–38

C–39

C–40

C-41

4 INTERIOR ACCESSORIES

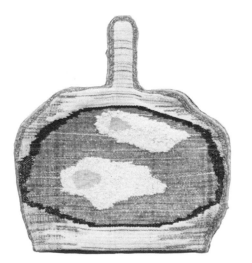

4–1. Frying pan tea cosy by Barbara De Peaux. The inside padding is commercial insulating material; photo courtesy of the artist.

4–2. Teapot tea cosy by Barbara De Peaux; photograph courtesy of the artist.

Art should not be separated from life. It should be there, integrated in our daily experience, in the constant use of everyday objects. "Art is not a plaything, but a necessity, and its essence, form, is not a decorative adjustment, but a cup into which life can be poured and lifted to the lips and be tasted"—Rebecca West; *Black Lamb & Gray Falcon.*

Functional objects can be a joy to use, influence our mood, and appeal to our senses. Like clothing accessories, interior accessories add spirited touches of fun to the interior environ-

ment. The tea cosies (Figures 4–1 and 4–2) illustrate an artist's conception of functional things; they remind us of the Art Deco of the Twenties and the Pop Art of the Sixties. As a true craftsman, the weaver used techniques which best interpreted her imaginative ideas to transform humble objects into notable artistic designs, with the aid of free-form tapestry techniques, thoughtful mixtures of yarns, and cardwoven bands as edges. Shaped on the loom, the tea cosies are filled with commercial padding which insulates the heat.

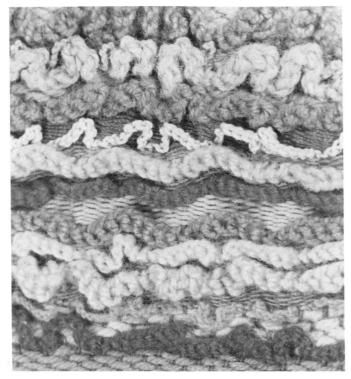

4–3. Detail of pillow made with chained loops by Helga Zirkel.

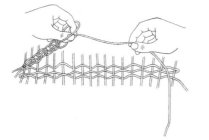

4–3a. Technique of chained loops, used as a decorative weft effect amid tabby picks.

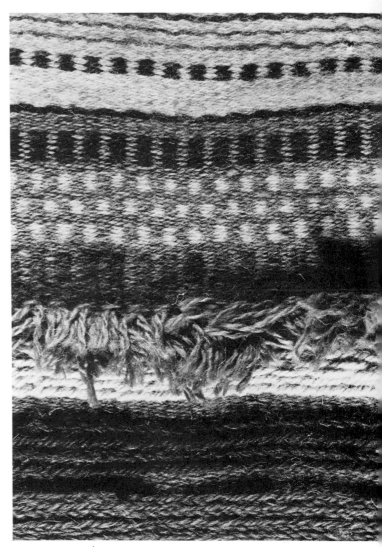

4–4. Detail of floor pillow incorporating bound weave, soumak, and rya techniques.

PILLOWS

Pillows can make colorful accents in a room and are projects which can lead weavers in many directions. Colors and textures can be freely combined, without the fear of overpowering a room's decor, since pillows are relatively small objects.

Bound weaving, rya knots (made into fringes), chained and pulled-up loops, embroidery weaves, knotted loops which completely or partially cover a surface, a pattern weave in undulating twill, and many color-and-weave effects are all used successfully in these weavings. An especially intriguing technique is shown in Figure 4–6. First, three separate bands twice the length of the pillow are woven. Then the basic pillow cover is woven to half of its final length, after which the warp ends from the separate bands are inserted into the warp on which the underlying pillow cover is being woven. When the underlying cover is finished, taken off the loom, and folded, the bands are wrapped around it, interlacing with each other, and their ends are sewn into its seams. The same weaver also uses many weights of wool in fine nuances of colors to achieve a softly rich surface texture on pillows by knotting rya loops over a rod (Figure 4–7).

4–5. Floor pillow by Astra Kleinhofs-Strobel; photograph by Robert Cooper.

4–6. Pillow with interlacing woven bands by Sandra Ullman; photo courtesy of the artist.

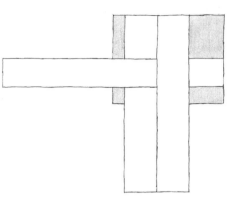

4–6a. Pillow with unfolded bands.
The dark areas show the basic pillow.

4–7. Pillow with heavy rya loops knotted over a rod, by Sandra Ullman; photo courtesy of the artist.

4–7a. Pillow with looped surface decoration, by Sandra Ullman; photo courtesy of artist.

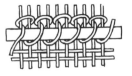

4–7b. Technique of making rya loops over a rod.

4–8. Pillow woven with handspun yarns by Mary Libby Neiman. Overspinning results in knobs for surface texture. All photos of this technique by Michel Ditlove.

An even more unusual way of enhancing surface texture is to make use of the properties of handspun yarn. The weaver uses a Turkish spindle to make knobs in the yarn; these expand into curls when woven into the handspun yarn of the pillow. The rich wool warp also forms a long double fringe, created when the single strip of weaving is doubled over to form the pillow (Figure 4–8)

4–8c, d, e, f. Four steps in spinning wool fibers on a Turkish spindle to make the knobs in the yarn.

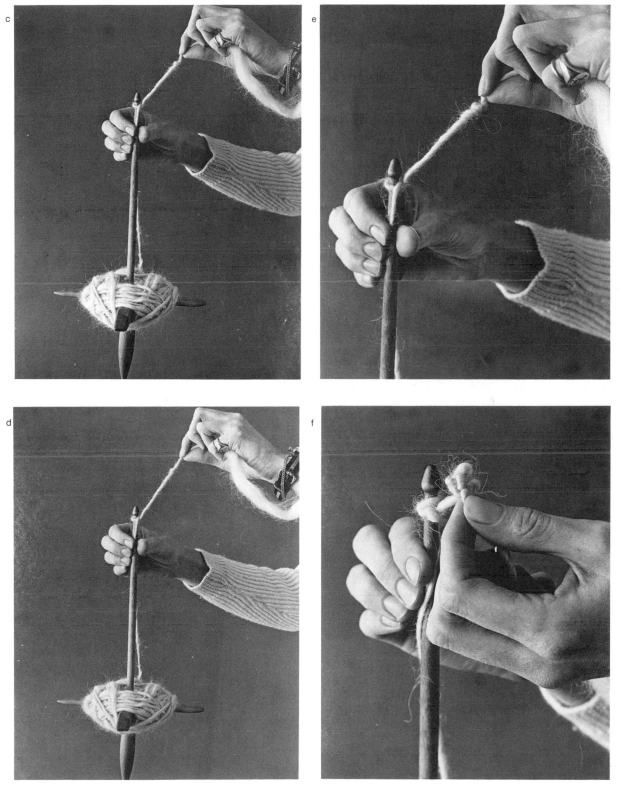

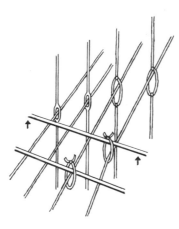

4–9. Device for pulling up warp threads to make pockets in tubular double-weave pillow, which is shown in color on page 73 (Figure C–19).

4–9a. Draft for Figure C–19.

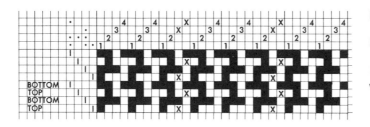

A pillow can be shaped and stuffed in various ways. The pillow shown in color on page 73 (Figure C–19) is woven in a rectangular shape with stuffed tubular pockets. The whole piece is folded over a basic pillow stuffing, then sewn at the sides, and both ends of its warp tied together to make the fringe. The pockets are made in tubular weave, but the ridges between them are a one-layer tabby surface. To create this effect, two out of the four warp ends at the ridges are threaded through long-eyed heddles so that they can be picked up out of the pocket pattern at every second pick (Figure 4–9).

To do this, first mark the spots on the warp with a thread where the ridges are planned. When threading the harnesses, plan for harnesses 1 and 2 to be the top layer, and harnesses 3 and 4 the bottom layer. Where you want to close the tubes to make the pockets (in this pillow it was only at four points), thread the warp on harness 3 and harness 4 through the special long-eyed heddles, which allows them to be woven normally and also to be pulled up when needed on the surface. After sleying the double-weave warp in the usual way, with two threads in each dent, and tying it to the apron rod, attach a leash to each of the ridge threads of harnesses 3 and 4 between the harness and the beater. Then slip a thin dowel stick through all leashes of harness 3 and another through all leashes of harness 4. Tie the two rods loosely so that they don't fall out. This leash is also called a "doup."

4–10. Black-and-white cushion in color-and-weave effect by Sandra Ullman; photo courtesy of the artist.

Then weave:

(1) Raise harness 1, also lifting the harness 3 ridge thread by the leash and weave (face pick).

(2) Drop the leash and raise harnesses 1, 2, and 3 and weave (back pick).

(3) Raise harness 2, also lifting the harness 4 ridge threads by the leashes and weave (face pick).

(4) Drop the leashes and raise harnesses 1, 2, and 4 and weave (back pick).

(5) Repeat until the pockets are as long as wanted.

(6) Raise harnesses 1 and 2 and stuff the pockets. Close pockets with four plain-weave picks, connecting the two layers.

(7) Repeat from beginning for twice the length of the pillow.

Five other pillows shown here (Figures 4–10 to 4–14), each in a different weave and method, show the enormous variety in which these attractive interior accents can be made.

4–11. Wool cushion in undulating twill by Stana Coleman. Threading and warp are the same as the draft in Figure 3–6a.

4-12. Supplementary warp threads form a warp-faced design in pillow by Stana Coleman; photo by Robert Fields.

4-13. Tapestry weave in small pillow top from Vlasti, Greece.

4-14. Wool pillow top in "embroidery weave" made at the American Farm School in Greece (see Figure 2-8).

BASKETS

A technique which lends itself to the making of charming interior accessories is basketry. A useful and attractive art from earliest prehistoric times, basketry through the centuries and throughout the world is a native craft of all cultures, forerunner of weaving and pottery. All forms of basketry employ the interlacing of two sets of elements, related to warp and weft, although the process is not done on a loom. The contemporary craftsman, ever in search of new ideas, has adopted basketry as a creative craft closely related to his feeling for natural materials and his concept of three-dimensional design. Inevitably the weaver turns to fibers such as wool, cotton, jute, and silk in place of the reeds, bamboos, canes, and grasses of traditional baskets.

An immense variety of shapes and forms is possible, and the intricate and beautiful designs of plaited, woven, twined, and coiled baskets can inspire the weaver who studies this new field. Figure 4–15 illustrates a beautiful contemporary basket of classical form. Fine yarn is coiled around a core of handspun

wool, which allows the core to provide the principal texture. The lid is fitted perfectly to a bowl sensitively shaped in the process of coiling. The form culminates in a loop that holds long strands of the core material, meticulously wrapped with gleaming silk threads to provide additional decorative elements. Figure 4–16 shows an equally handsome basket by the same artist with feathers wrapped into the rim of the elegantly shaped lip of the open top. For a detailed discussion of various coiling techniques see Chapter 2 and the mariposa knot in Figure 5–15a.

Baskets, too, go with a child's way of life. Small coiled baskets in colored wool are sturdy enough to hold many treasures of marbles, stones, buttons or shells. Older children can be encouraged to weave them themselves, and imagination can provide not only for their use, but also for their decoration. In figure 4–17 the two coiled baskets are made from colored wool with a core of jute; the top of one is decorated with little feathers woven into the last row.

4–15. Coiled wool basket with lid, by Kathy Malec; photo courtesy of the artist.

4–16. Coiled wool basket with feather decoration, by Kathy Malec; photo courtesy of the artist.

4–17. Two small coiled baskets for children's treasures, by Else Regensteiner.

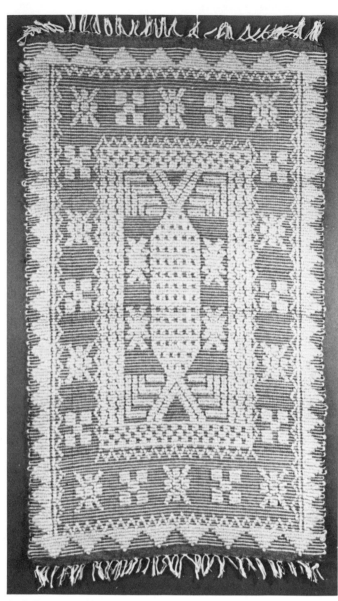

4–18. Traditional Greek design in *skulato* technique; collection of Lana and Robert Fields, photo by Robert Fields.

THROWS AND SPREADS

An interesting technique for a great variety of accessories, such as spreads, throw pillows, and cushions, is a method of pulling up loops without knotting them as one would in a rug Figures 4–20 and 4–20a illustrate pulled-up loops of heavy wool on a flat background. Figures 4–18 and 4–21 show two textiles made in Greece, where the method is called *skulato*. One piece (Figure 4–18) is in a traditional design and the other is a contemporary adaptation of a pebble floor from the excavation of Pella in northern Greece. The design is carried out in wool loops on a black-and-white background, which gives a gray effect.

The shuttle is thrown into the tabby shed and then, with the fingers, the weft is pulled up between the warp threads, and, in accordance with the pattern design, looped over a rod (see Figure 4–20). Three finer tabby threads are thrown between each row of the loops and beaten down very hard before the rod is removed from the previous row.

Many variations are possible with this technique. Some weavers prefer to use a crochet hook for pulling up the loops, and the height and density of the pile can be controlled by using rods of different sizes and by throwing more tabbies between the rows of loops Since the loops are not knotted, and therefore not as secure as in rya or flossa pile weaves (see Chapter 3), the weave must be very tight and firm to prevent the loops from pulling out. In the Greek examples the warp is set in fine cotton, 20 threads per inch. The weft is a homespun wool, used double on the shuttle for the pile, single for the tabbies. Even though this technique is very old and has been used in nearly all countries, it is fascinating for the contemporary weaver because of the textural possibilities and the wide scope it offers for free and abstract, geometric, or realistic designs.

4–19. Blue loops on yellow background make an effective design in *skulato* pillow by Sylvia Palazzolo.

4–20. Mary Demoula weaving *skulato* fabric on loom in Greece; photo by the author.

4–20a. Technique of *skulato*.

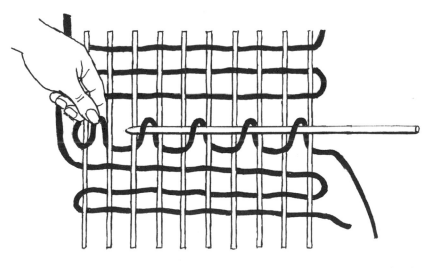

4–21. Contemporary design by Else Regensteiner, adapted from pebble floor in excavation site at Pella, in northern Greece, woven by Athina Sopholoye; photo by John W. Rosenthal. In collection of Nancy C. Newman.

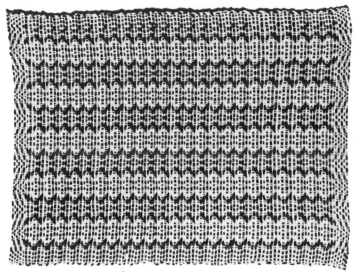

4–22. Placemat in Star of Bethlehem pattern, designed by Else Regensteiner for the American Farm School in Greece.

4–22a. Draft. This shows the rising shed, with natural warp and black weft. Both mats (4–22 and 4–23) are woven lengthwise on the loom.

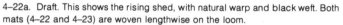

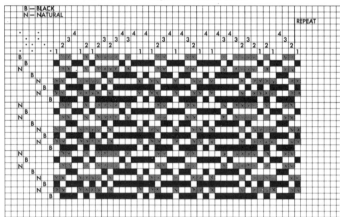

PLACEMATS

Even such small textiles as placemats can provide notable interior accents. They have to be designed to lie flat on the table, so the relationship between the size of warp and weft yarns, which determines the setting in the reed, becomes very important. In Figure 4–22, number 5 cotton with a heavy weft was set at 18 threads per inch. If a heavier weft were used, the warp would be set fewer threads to the inch. In Figure 4–23 a similar size linen thread was used 20 ends per inch with a lighter weft.

A pattern weave can be a simple and effective way to design placemats. In Figure 4–22 the traditional Star of Bethlehem threading was woven in a 1/3 twill with four threads on each shuttle (white on one, black on the other) and no tabby treadling. The other mat, Figure 4–23, is woven of black-and-white linen in a three-tie Summer and Winter threading, which gives the surface an all-over twill appearance. There are three binding threads used in this rotation instead of the usual two. This weave is similar to the one discussed in relation to the upholstery fabric in Figure 3–14.

4–23. Black-and-white linen placemat in Summer and Winter weave by Margaret Sheppard.

4–23a. Draft. The warp is natural linen; the weft is natural linen in the hem and alternating black and natural linen in the pattern.

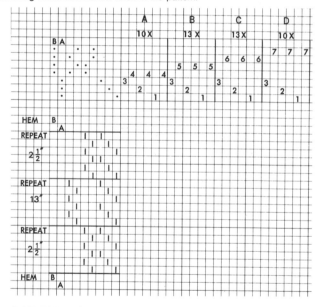

CAT ENVIRONMENT

An environment for a pet can also serve as a sculptural accent in a room. A dog often has his own house outdoors, but a cat's home can be designed for the living room. The one shown here is a three-dimensional tubular weaving, designed so that the fringes which form the curtain are part of the warp. Because cats always crawl into paper bags, the shape is planned so a paper bag fits inside. The bag is not only an inducement to the cat, but also prevents the weaving from being scratched.

The shape was completely formed on the loom, with some additional threads laid in for decoration. An armature of wire, from clothes hangers, on a plywood base was made to support the weaving, before the bag was inserted. Diagrams 4–24a and b illustrate the construction of the armature and how to shape the weaving on the loom.

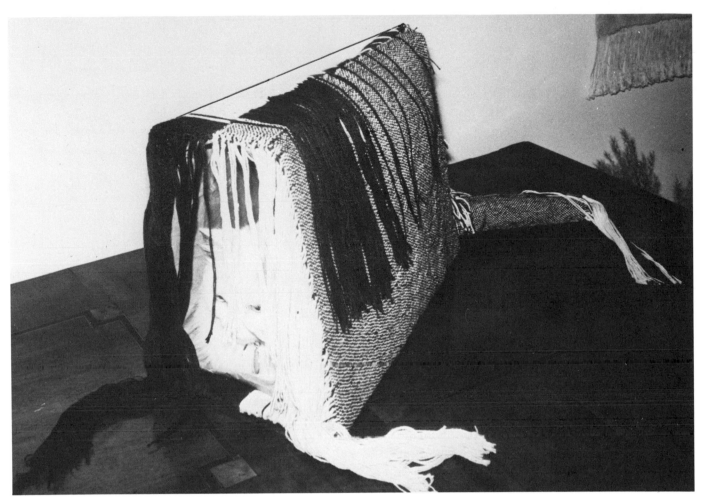

4–24. Cat environment by Lynda Y. Cannon; collection of the author.

4–24a. Diagram of armature.

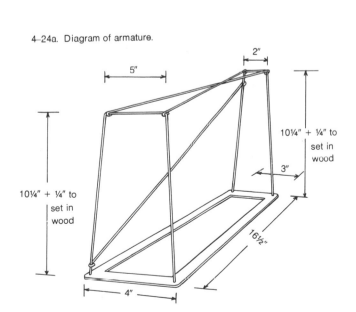

5"

2"

10¼" + ¼" to set in wood

3"

10¼" + ¼" to set in wood

16½"

4"

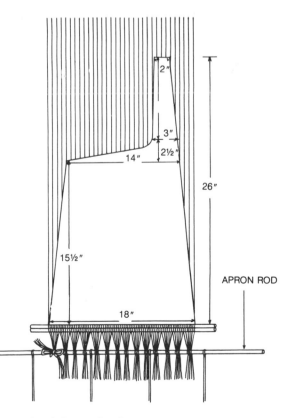

2"

3"

2½"

14"

26"

15½"

APRON ROD

18"

4–24b. Diagram for tubular weaving shape.

HANGING CHAIRS AND HAMMOCKS

Hammocks and hanging chairs can bring interior design out of doors. Used on patios or in gardens and woods, they are perfect companions of today's style of living. They can be taken along on a picnic or used inside on permanent supports. The chair illustrated in Figure 4–25 is simply a rug woven in straight and broken twill, with various color sequences giving the design. The warp is a rough-spun heavy flax set at 4 ends per inch, 14 inches wide. The weft is acrylic yarn used fourfold.

The warp for this piece is planned to extend on both ends to a point where additional support could be added without sacrificing strength. Warp thread is used for one-half inch of tabby, followed by another half inch of twill weave. To provide a place for the wooden arms, slit sections are woven on four threads each. This is followed by another half inch of twill.

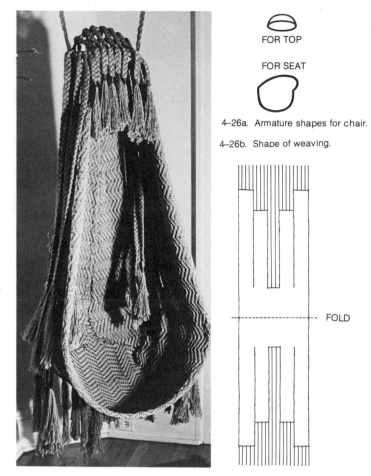

FOR TOP

FOR SEAT

4–26a. Armature shapes for chair.

4–26b. Shape of weaving.

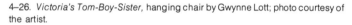

FOLD

4–26. *Victoria's Tom-Boy-Sister,* hanging chair by Gwynne Lott; photo courtesy of the artist.

4–25. Orange and gold hanging chair by Betty Lukins; photo courtesy of the artist.

4–25a. Diagram showing woven patterns, slit sections, and inclusion of rings.

As the pattern and color sequences continue, two rings are included, separated by 1 1/2 inches of weaving. The weaving continues 12 more inches to the center where the entire process is reversed. The arms are sections of one-inch dowel fastened by double-pointed screws to ready-made birch door pulls. The balls on the ropes are larger birch pulls which have been fully drilled.

The chair back is created by sewing bands, woven in a warp-faced strip on the four harness loom to give an effect similar to cardweaving. Threads which are used as weft in the chair are arranged in colored stripes as a closely set warp. A twill and herringbone combination is threaded in the heddles. The treadling is a regular 2/2 reversed twill. Knotting and braiding provide a finish for the ends.

A most interesting project is the hanging chair in Figure 4–26. Many small mock-up models of the shape were made before the final design was determined, just as weavers make samples to decide on a fabric. Then the steel frame is specially welded according to the design specifications. The chair is woven on the loom with jute upholstery cord for warp and a strong rug linen for weft, in a reverse twill pattern in a straight piece of weaving (Figure 4–26b). After weaving, the fabric is folded in the center around a steel frame of two parts, one for the seat and one for the top. Then the piece is seamed to complete the shape. The warp ends are left to form the decorative braids, enriched by added linen.

4–27. Hammock by Gwynne Lott; photo by the artist.

4–27a. Detail.

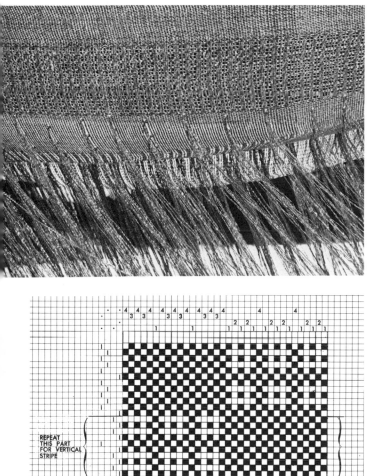

4–28. *Katari,* twined and braided swing by Gwynne Lott; photo by the artist.

4–28a. Detail.

REPEAT THIS PART FOR VERTICAL STRIPE

4–27b. Draft for Swedish-lace weave. Only the first part of the treadling is used.

4–28b. Technique of twining.

The hammock in Figure 4–27 is woven lengthwise with the warp stripe in a Swedish-lace weave. In other words, the pattern is a Swedish-lace weave threaded in blocks so that one block is an open lace pattern and the other is a plain weave. The two blocks can be reversed by changes in the treadling. When the treadling remains the same (as here) the plain and the lace blocks produce vertical bands, or stripes, along the warp. The warp, in a very strong material—rayon tire belting—is threaded at both ends through holes in mahogany rods and knotted to make the supports. The hanging fringes are attached during the weaving with rya knots.

Katari, the third project made by this weaver, is a twined and braided swing made off the loom from strong jute upholstery cord on steel rings. After suspending the strong warp from an overhead support, the swing is made in weft twining and braiding techniques, which gives the design a pleasing variety of vertical, horizontal and open bands. Long fringes of the heavy jute cord are added afterwards to the wrapped steel rings as decoration.

5 TOYS

Weaving can have many moods—the weaver can express his sense of humor and delight in his craft by applying them to the happy task of creating children's toys. A child's play, built upon discovery and creative imagination, is perhaps the most important expression of inherent qualities of human character and helps establish basic values. Mechanized toys stifle this urge for spontaneous exploration, and thus are less creative than those which encourage active participation. The simpler the toy is, the more actively stimulating it can be. The weaver can create toys which combine simplicity with good taste, tactile appeal with classic forms, fun with affection, and art with function. Long before mechanized toys were invented, dolls, balls, and stuffed animals helped children to invent and discover their own world—the rag doll and the teddy bear have been favorites for a long time, because they can be used to imitate adult activities, while at the same time permitting the child to endow them with any quality, characteristic, and activity his imagination provides at a particular stage of his development.

In the making of all toys, attention must be paid to the fact that they not only have to be attractive enough to delight a child, but also practical enough to make their washing and cleaning an easy task for the adult. The rougher the wear, as in balls and stuffed animals that sit on the floor, the sturdier the weave construction should be.

DOLLS

Imagination is the key to a creative approach, in conception as well as in purpose. A doll can be just as expressive as a sculpture. Toys which delight the eye, challenge the senses, and show understanding of human nature are well within the reach of the weavers' craft, and are certainly more valuable for the child than dolls which mechanically reflect childhood seen from an adult's point of view.

Tubular weaves are ideal techniques for making dolls and stuffed animals. The tubular dolls in Peruvian style (Figure 5–1) are woven from a diagram the size of the doll, in a tubular double-weave tapestry technique. Since the dolls are stuffed on the loom during the weaving process, the two layers of warp are held at different tensions—the top warp hung over the back beam and weighted with bags of gravel, the other threaded in the normal way. The weaving is worked up from the toes in a flat-weave, slit technique which makes three sections. The protruding warp ends are later wrapped to make the toes and fingers, and the closed areas darned with matching yarns.

The legs are woven in two tubes and stuffed. Parts of the warp on either side are left unwoven until the place where the fingers begin, and the weaving is shaped from there on upward for the torso and the head (and, in the girl doll, for the skirt). Warp

5-1. Tubular dolls in Peruvian style by Rosemarie Last. Also shown in color on page 55 (Figure C-15).

5-1a. Diagram for weaving.

5-2. Tubular doll by Sylvia Palazzolo; body 2-inches wide, arms and legs 1-inch each. The doll is 15 inches long. In collection of the author.

threads for the teeth and part of the eyes are left unwoven and wrapped afterwards. To make a neat finish, the finger and toe warps are doubled back and pulled up through their own wrapping.

All three dolls shown in color on page 55 (Figure C-13) are woven in tubular weave but the dress and wig of the Indian doll in the center is woven separately. The dress can be taken off and put on the doll for play. In the other dolls the clothing is a permanent part of the structure.

Dolls made exclusively for play are shown in imaginative forms in Figures 5-2 to 5-4. They are all tubular. The doll in Figure 5-2 is made completely in one piece without any sewing.

It is very flexible because the two layers of the tubes are interwoven at all the joints. The gold wool warp is left as fingers and toes, knotted at one shoulder for epaulets, and wrapped around the torso for the other shoulder as a scarf. The hair also consists of warp ends with the two layers tied together. The eyes, nose, and mouth are embroidered afterwards.

The whimsical doll in Figure 5-3, which is a boy on one side and a girl on the other, and the one called Santa, remind me of a doll I had as a child that lived happily dangling from a hook inside our tall grandfather's clock. It was a distinct pleasure for me, when a small child, to open the door, take out the toy for play, and carefully return it to its place afterwards.

5-3. *Hippie-Baby* (boy side) by Libby Crawford.   5-3a. *Hippie-Baby* (girl side) by Libby Crawford.

5-4. *Santa,* tubular double weave, red on one side, beige on the other side, by Libby Crawford.

5–5. *Mollie Brown* by Joyce Miller.

5–6. *Willie Make It* and *I Am Me.* Dolls by Joyce Miller.

5–7. *Baby Doll* by Joyce Miller.

The four dolls shown in Figures 5–5, 5–6, and 5–7 are the work of a single weaver. *Mollie Brown* is woven on a gold silk warp which also forms long macramé hair that is mixed with red and pink wools. *Willie Make It* has a black wool warp with cowhair and wool weft, while his companion is an unflattering self portrait of the weaver, woven on linen warp with handspun wool, handspun silk, and handspun mohair for weft. The weft of *Baby Doll* is handspun polyester fiber, and the warp is a soft tan silk yarn, so that the doll is machine washable in cool water as well as being a soft tactile pleasure for an infant. *Red Riding Hood* (Figure 5–8) is a three-layered construction which needs six harnesses. The hood and the cape were woven on the third layer (which is below the other two) simultaneously with the tubes for the body. The third layer was connected at the shoulders to the tubular layers. The doll is made from perle cotton in the manner of the other dolls.

Toys need not be only for children; they can also be companions for adults. *Yarnella* (Figure 5–9) is a life-size person of fiber, who rides in cars and actually receives letters and presents from her friends. She was woven on two warps, one blue and one pink, in tapestry technique, and stuffed with dacron. *Rosie,* shown in color on page 55 (Figure C–14) is a sculptural doll who can wear her head or take it off like a hat. She is woven in tubular weave on the loom in separate parts that are all removable and interchangeable. Imaginative adornments were added with crochet, soumak, rya knots, and fringes.

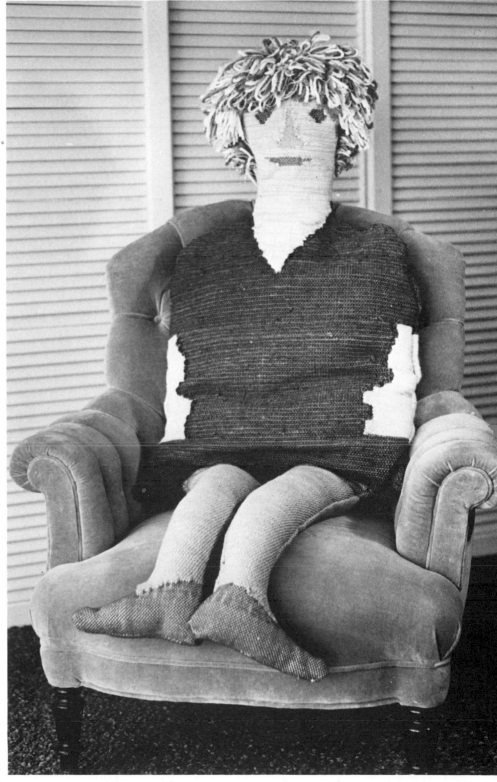

5–8. *Red Riding Hood*, triple-weave doll by Judith Gordon; collection of the author.

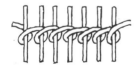

5–10. The technique of soumak, shown over one warp thread; and over four, under two warp threads.

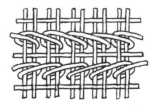

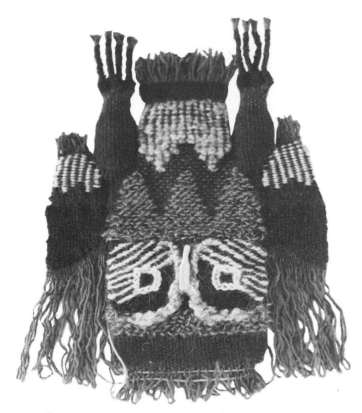

5–11a. Tapestry owl, stuffed and finished.

5–12. Caterpillar by Susan Feulner; collection of the author.

5–11. Tapestry owl, shown as woven on the loom, by Jo Le Mieux; photos courtesy of the artist.

TAPESTRY OWL AND OTHER STUFFED ANIMALS

In contrast to the dolls, the owl is woven upside down, though also in a tubular tapestry technique. The warp is a tightly twisted single-ply wool/nylon yarn. One hundred and forty-four ends are set 16 per inch (threaded 3, 3, 2, 3, 3, 2) in a 6-dent reed and woven with selective warp groupings to make the separate tubes of the wings, legs, and torso. Other techniques are added, such as soumak (eyebrows) and chain weave (outlining the eyes). The beak is a separate strand of doubled linen rug warp that is wrapped, arched, and added before the tube is stuffed and sewn.

To make the owl sit firmly on its tail and grasp a stick in its talons, the wool stuffing is supported with stiff shoe leather in the tail and small wooden dowels in the legs. For the talons, florists' wire is laid over the toe warp threads and wrapped together with the warp.

Simple tubular shapes, enriched with rya knots, can make cuddly, flexible toys like the caterpillar in Figure 5–12. Not all tube shapes are made in tubular weave; the snake in Figure 5–13 is a sample of patterns of four-harness overshot in the Colonial coverlet threading Catalpa Flowers. The warp is black 18/2 worsted, and the weft is wool in many bright colors. Tubular weave does not allow for such a great variety of patterns as this toy has, so it is woven in a long strip that is later sewn together on the underside, turned, and stuffed. Afterwards, rya fringes and beady eyes are added to decorate the head. Two tubular sections in plain weave form the mouth. A long, bright tongue of yarn and a tasseled and beaded tail complete this lively and attractive toy.

5–13. Snake in many patterns by Libby Crawford.

5–14. Toy for fingers, ears, and nose, by Joyce Miller.

5–15. *Geometric Variables*, constructive toy by Sylvia Palazzolo.

GAMES AND BALLS

A woven game in soft handspun home-dyed wool appeals to the tactile sense and is a challenge to the ears and nose. It is woven in tubular pockets (much like the pillow in Figure C–19 on page 73) which contain items of varied textures and sizes—bells, marbles, pebbles, pieces of wood, rings, paper, and something nice to smell. Small children are intrigued, and older children challenged, when told to name the contents buried in the pockets only with the help of their other senses of hearing, smell, and touch.

Six interlocking geometric figures, in a basketry technique combining wrapping and stitching, make another creative and imaginative toy (Figure 5–15). A child can take it apart and reconstruct it in many ways. The core is a heavy jute rope wrapped with wool of various colors. The geometric forms are made in any pattern by connecting the coils with a lace or mariposa knot as shown in the drawing.

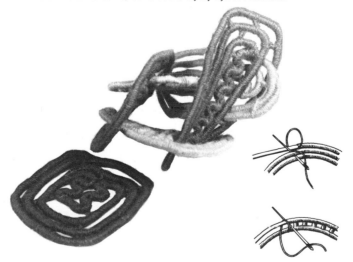

5–15a. Technique for basketry wrapping and stitching. The connecting stitch is the lace, or mariposa, knot.

Every child has a ball. It is perhaps the most basic of toys. Yet, even with such a simple shape, the weaver's imagination can transform the toy into a work of art. The use of synthetic yarns for the weaving and a foam rubber stuffing for the inside guarantees the usefulness of these balls for a long time.

The ball shown in color on page 54 (Figure C–11) is woven in tapestry technique, using 4-ply knitting yarn as warp in a 10-dent reed, which makes a very flexible material. As shown in Figure 5–16, the free-form tapestry actually covers a bouncing ball, and is based on the construction of a real baseball, with two curvilinear pieces sewn together. Since each half is woven on a different warp, a great range of patterns in many colors is possible. The fabric was woven 11 inches wide and then the pattern was pinned on top and cut out twice, for the two pieces. Except for the last part of the stitching, after the ball was inserted, the pieces were sewn together by machine.

5–17. Icosahedron "ball" by Sally Posner; photo courtesy of the artist.

5–17a. Wrapping each triangle with weaving.

5–16. Pattern for the woven "baseball" shown in color on page 54 (Figure C–11). The pattern piece is 3½ inches wide at its narrowest point and 6 inches wide at the widest point of the two ends. Altogether, it is 24 inches long and creates a ball with a 9-inch diameter. Two pieces are needed.

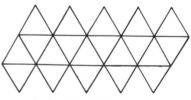

5–17b. Joining the triangles.

5–17c. The completed shape is a rigid self-supporting structure.

The multi-surfaced ball in Figure 5–17 is composed of woven triangles in a variety of textures, colors, and weaves, which are stitched together over a rigid shape, called an icosahedron, to make an object that is interesting to touch and play with. Icosahedron comes from the Greek stem *eikosi* (twenty) and *hedron* (surface), and the ball, each facet of which is woven with natural dyed yarns in yellow and green, is constructed of 20 equilateral triangles. Set up side by side for the width of the loom, each triangle is woven in a different pattern. The following directions are kindly supplied by Sally Posner:

(1) Weave the fabrics. Cut each shape, then stay-stitch the edges to prevent fraying.

(2) Cut 20 equilateral triangles from heavy cardboard, all the same size.

(3) Glue fabric to cardboard triangles, turning edges under on back (Figure 5–17a).

(4) Arrange the triangles in the desired color scheme as shown in Figure 5–17b.

(5) Sew the triangles together by hand with an overhand stitch along adjacent edges.

(6) Then close up the shape, by bringing the upper row of triangles and lower row of triangles together around each vertex.

(7) Sew up remaining seams. An icosahedron is a rigid shape and needs no further reinforcement (Figure 5–17c).

Triangles, such as those used for the multi-textured and patterned ball, can be made by weaving straight fabric on the loom and cutting and sewing the triangles according to a paper pattern. Other triangles can be shaped directly on the loom in various ways.

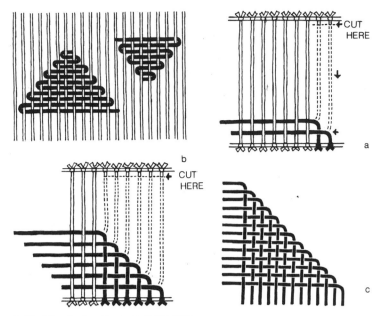

5–18. Triangle shapes woven on the loom.

5–18a, b, c. Three steps in creating a large triangle out of warp threads only, in a technique related to plaiting.

A paper pattern can be cut into the desired shape and laid directly under the warp. The shape is then traced on the warp threads with a soft pencil or felt pen, and the weft follows the outlines of the shape by dropping warp threads not needed on the sides (Figure 5–18). After the weaving is completed, these warp threads are cut off and darned back into the fabric, or left hanging as decorative fringes. On a wide warp several triangles can be woven simultaneously across the width of the warp.

Another method is to plan one large 90-degree triangle so that the warp itself is used as the weft, and the triangular shape forms itself from only one set of elements. This is related to the technique of plaiting. Use yarns which are somewhat bulky or fuzzy, such as knitting wool or mohair. The width of the warp forms one short side of the triangle, and only one triangle can be woven at a time. Plan the warp so that the length is 1/3 longer than the width of the warp. Warp the loom in the usual manner for a plain-weave threading (a two-harness loom or a frame may be used). Tie warp to the back and front apron sticks in the usual manner. When ready to weave, cut one thread near the back apron on the right side, and pull it toward the front out of the heddle and the reed. Open the shed and weave this thread into the warp (Figure 5–18a). Cut the next thread from the same side in the same manner and weave into the opposite plain-weave shed. Continue until all warp threads have been woven in (Figure 5–18b). The triangle has formed itself, with fringes on two short sides and a plain diagonal edge on the long side (Figure 5–18c).

WALL HANGINGS AND THREE-DIMENSIONAL STARS

Wall hangings and mobiles can surround a child with joy and fun as much as toys can. Even infants love to watch mobiles turn and sway in the air. The charming *Bird in a Cage,* shown in color on page 51 (Figure C–6) is a hanging for a child's room, made with warmth and humor. It is woven in a tubular, three-layer weave on six harnesses. The top and bottom of the cage is woven as one layer but the bars of the cage are formed by

5–19. *Owls in the Woods,* wall hanging by Carol Weston; photo by Richard Olson.

leaving two layers of unwoven warp threads around the bird and perch. The figures are woven on the middle layer, with harnesses 1 and 2 held up out of the way. The hanging is given support by weaving thin sticks in across the top and bottom.

The fish mobile, shown in color on page 51 (Figure C–8), is a combination of pin weaving (see Figure 2–16 on page 33) and driftwood. The weaving, inspired by the natural shape of the driftwood, is made on a form cut to the shape of the wood, then is glued onto the wood.

A hanging showing owls in the most varied weaves and techniques is created by appliquéing the birds to the sheer and partly unwoven background, letting them nestle on real twigs and woven-in branches (Figure 5–19). Interesting supports, woven fringes, and wool tassels unify the hanging, which would delight not only children but adults as well.

5–20a. Drawing of mobile.

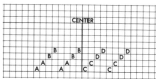

5–20d. Draft for using a single color.

5–20b. Draft.

5–20e. Draft for using two colors.

5–20c. Draft showing threading and tie-up for eight harnesses.

5–20f. Draft for using four colors.

5–20. Four-pointed star mobile by Georgia Suiter.

Funny Face, shown in color on page 76 (Figure C–26) is a small hanging using the supplementary warp technique, described in Chapter 3. The textured background is a basic warp in many green shades; the supplementary pattern threads are brown wool. In this hanging the pattern blocks are used to form the features of the face, and the remaining unwoven supplementary warp is pulled together at the top, while part of it creates loops of hair. Both warps mingle for the bottom fringe.

Four-pointed star mobile

Three-dimensional mobiles in the form of four- or six-pointed stars, with their bright colors, tight or lacy weaves, balls, beads, or tassels can be exciting projects for weavers and a delight to children. They can be made large or small, wide or narrow, and can be used not only in a child's room but for many other purposes as well. As tiny ornaments they might grace a Christmas tree, or, made with tinkling bells, they might sway on a porch in the wind.

Four-harness weave Weaving these mobiles is easy. Several color variations can be planned for the warp, which must have a number of warp threads per inch suitable for a double cloth (twice the number usually used for one layer) and two threads sleyed through the same dent. This determines whether the warp colors will be the same for all four sides, whether they will appear opposite each other, or whether they will change to another set of colors for each side. The variations are as follows:

(1) Warp threads can be all one color (Figure 5–20d).

(2) Two colors of warp threads can be threaded in one sequence to the center and then reversed for the other half (see Figure 5–20b and 5–20c).

(3) Warp threads can be in four colors, two colors threaded to the center, and two different colors for the other half (Figure 5–20f).

The principle of the weave is that the two layers of the double weave interchange in the center in the following method (Figures 5–20b and 5–21):

(1) Use two different colors, each one wound on a separate shuttle. Start color a from the left selvage.

(2) Raise harness 2, weave to the center, and bring shuttle up out of the warp. Change shed to raise harnesses 1–2–3. Insert shuttle again and weave to right selvage.

(3) Change to harnesses 1–2–4, weave color a from right to center, bring shuttle out, and change shed to raise harness 1. Reinsert and weave across to left selvage.

(4) Starting at the opposite (right) side, repeat the above steps with color b. Throughout the design, colors a and b must start from their own opposite sides. This means that the weft color starts on the side of the warp color which is the first one to be raised for the top layer. In Figures 5–20d and e, this means starting color a on the left side. (In 5–20e, this results in solid colors alternating in each spoke; in 5–20d, color a will be solid in two spokes and mixed with color b in the other two spokes.) In Figure 5–20f more mixtures are obtained. Many other variations in color combinations can be created because the weft colors can be changed continuously as long as the correct rotation is maintained.

Important note: After a few beginning picks a narrow supporting stick or dowel must be inserted for *each* of the two layers

5–21. The principle of the weave when using two colors, a and b in weft.

104

5–22. Six-pointed star mobile. Also shown in color on page 56 (Figure C–16).

5–22a. Draft. The color distribution for the six-pointed star is: yellow—harnesses 1 and 4; blue—harnesses 2 and 5; orange—harnesses 3 and 6.

5–22b. The three layers shown on the loom, with color distribution; drawings by Lynda Cannon.

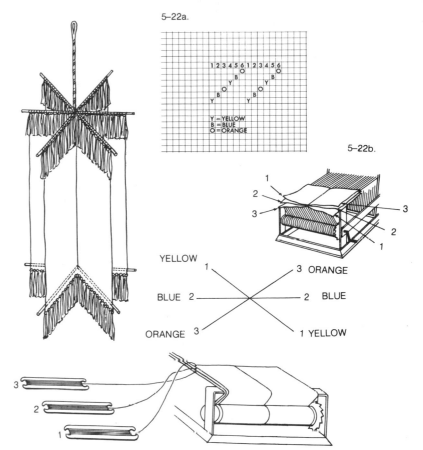

5–22a.

5–22b.

YELLOW
BLUE 2
ORANGE 3

1 3 ORANGE
2 BLUE
1 YELLOW

5–22c. Rotation of shuttles.

along with the shuttle (also coming out at the center of the pick and going on through after the changing of the shed). This step must be repeated near the end of the hanging also. This is a permanent support for the hanging.

Eight-harness weave The same hanging can be made on eight harnesses where the two sides are threaded as blocks and the tie-up makes the changes automatically from the top layer to the bottom layer, and vice versa (Figure 5–20c). Two picks of one weft color are followed by two picks of the other weft color, and the shuttles may even start from the same side. Care must be taken that the weft will not close the layers on the sides; the proper method is shown in Figure 5–21.

Six-pointed star mobile

On six harnesses, a triple-layer fabric can be threaded, using two harnesses for each layer. Again, one thread from each layer must be sleyed through a single dent. This gives a six-pointed hanging (Figure 5–22). For this weave the colors alternate as follows:

harnesses 1 and 4—yellow
harnesses 2 and 5—blue
harnesses 3 and 6—orange

The three layers intersect at the center, as in the drawings, so that there are then six layers—two of each color (Figure 5–22b). As before, each spoke is one-half the width of the warp.
Picks 1 through 4 (yellow shuttle):

(1) Raise harness 1, weave from left to center, remove shuttle.

(2) Raise harnesses 1–2–3–5–6, reenter shuttle, and weave to right.

(3) Raise 2–3–4–5–6, weave back to center.

(4) Raise harness 4, weave to left selvage.

Picks 5 through 8 (blue shuttle):

(1) Raise 1–2–4, enter shuttle from left, remove at center.

(2) Raise 2–3–6, enter shuttle at center, pass to right.

(3) Raise 3–5–6, weave from right to center.

(4) Raise 1–4–5, weave from center to left.

Picks 9 through 12 (orange shuttle):

(1) Raise harnesses 1–2–3–4–5, enter shuttle from left, remove at center.

(2) Raise harness 3, enter shuttle at center, and weave to right.

(3) Raise harness 6, weave back to center.

(4) Raise harnesses 1–2–4–5–6, weave from center to left.

Important note: In the six-pointed hanging the shuttles can all start from the same side. To avoid weaving the edges closed, be careful not to cross the weft yarns at the edges. It helps to lay down the shuttles at the side of the loom in the order in which they are used, as shown in Figure 5–22c. Again, sticks or dowels must be woven through near the top and bottom of each layer, as permanent supports.

Simplified treadling for six-harness weave The directions already given will bring the colors of warp and weft to the points opposite each other. That is, each spoke will be a solid color as shown in Figure 5–22b. If the colors can be mixed, a simplified version can be treadled. The blue center layer, sandwiched between the top and bottom layer, can be treated as the second layer of the weave and woven straight from selvage to selvage, without the shuttle having to surface. Starting on the left side, weave as follows:
Yellow layer:

(1) Raise harness 1, weave to center.

(2) Bring shuttle out of warp.

(3) Raise harnesses 1–2–3–4–5, weave to right selvage.

(4) Raise harnesses 1–2–4–5–6, weave to center.

(5) Bring shuttle out of warp.

(6) Raise harness 4, weave to left selvage.

Blue layer:

(1) Weave from selvage to selvage 1–2–4.

(2) Weave from selvage to selvage 1–4–5.

(3) Repeat these two picks to make the weft even with the other layers.

Orange layer:

(1) Raise harnesses 1–2–3–4–5, weave to center.

(2) Raise harness 1, weave to selvage.

(3) Raise harness 4, weave to center.

(4) Raise harnesses 1–2–4–5–6, weave to selvage.

Textures, colors, and designs can be changed at will as long as the treadling sequence remains the same. The star hangings shown in this chapter can be woven on any warp which is set for a double or triple weave. Note: the dowels at the bottom of hangings may be eliminated if the weaver prefers a less rigid structure.

6 WALL HANGINGS AND SCULPTURAL WEAVING

As crafts have evolved during the last decade from the creation of functional objects to the status of fine art, the contemporary craftsman has become truly liberated. In many cases the functional and aesthetic, the useful and the abstract have merged, and woven fabrics have been created as fiber constructions meant primarily as statements of ideas and design conceptions. There are lively interchanges between fiber and metal, fiber and wood, fiber and clay. Weaving, stitching, wrapping and knotting go happily hand in hand. Three-dimensional fiber constructions and large two-dimensional hangings now find places not only in museums, but also in buildings such as banks, offices, and lobbies of apartment houses, where they give warmth and depth to bare walls, much as tapestries did in the Middle Ages for castles and churches.

The new freedom, challenging and exciting as it is, can degenerate into shoddy weaving, poor craftsmanship, and pretentious dishonesty, if it is not handled with artistic integrity. To withstand the test of time, art must be created with vision and understanding, by craftsmen who conceive their ideas not through imitation but through inspiration, whether it comes from sources within themselves, from sensitive observation, or from their own need for fulfilling expression.

Because of the structural freedom allowed the weaver, the creation of a wall hanging can be developed step by step as an artistic work. No idea should be abandoned after one attempt, because it might lead to an artwork that consists of a series of themes and variations. In wall hangings, no design repetition is needed, as in woven fabrics, but one idea inspires another. The mark of the artist is shown strongly in the conception and style of such works. Individualism, personality, and mastery of

technique can combine to make wall hangings into timeless pieces that will survive many superficial fashions of only momentary value.

An enormous variety of techniques are on hand to express the ideas of the artist-weaver. Techniques, however, are not ends in themselves, but only the means to achieve visual form for ideas. Feeling for tactile quality, awareness of the laws of design in nature, the study of the relationship of space to form—all are more important than mere concentration on complicated techniques. When intricacy and simplicity, superb craftsmanship and unsophisticated approach interact with each other they give excitement and force to a piece.

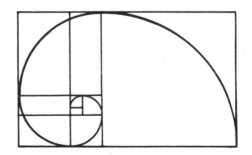

6–1. The chambered nautilus, a classical design proportion from nature.

TAPESTRY

The art of tapestry used to be a collaboration of painter and weaver in which the weaver adapted and executed the painter's cartoon, but now it is often entirely the work of one artist-weaver. Traditionally tapestries are woven from the back, with the cartoon turned horizontally for the weaving, and various techniques of joining the color areas can be employed depending on what suits the weaver best (Figure 6–2).

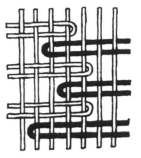

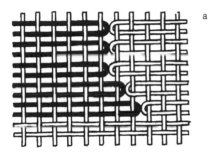

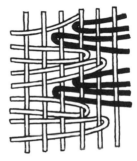

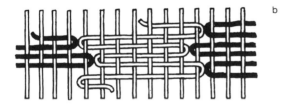

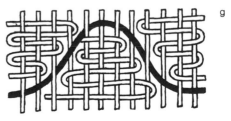

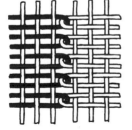

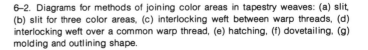

6–2. Diagrams for methods of joining color areas in tapestry weaves: (a) slit, (b) slit for three color areas, (c) interlocking weft between warp threads, (d) interlocking weft over a common warp thread, (e) hatching, (f) dovetailing, (g) molding and outlining shape.

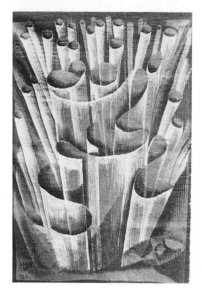

6–3. *Organdream*, wool and silk tapestry, 36 × 40 inches, by Monique Montandon; photo courtesy of the artist.

6–4. *Moon Goddess* by Wendell H. Teegarden; photo courtesy of the artist.

6–3a. Detail.

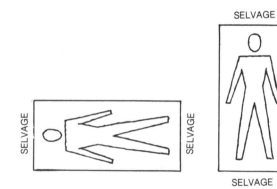

6–4a. Cartoon of any figured tapestry woven horizontally on loom.

6–4b. Design turned vertically, and hanging from selvage.

Monique Montandon of Switzerland, whose works are shown here and in color on page 78, displays mastery of the tapestry technique, a fine conception of design, and an inherent understanding of the blending of yarns and colors. *Organdream,* and her works shown in color, were designed and woven entirely by her, on a vertical loom (high warp) with 10 ends of cotton warp and 34 to 48 wefts of silk and wool per inch. These works vividly demonstrate that working in a traditional technique can give scope and freedom to the artist to express his creative vision and talent.

Traditional technique, with a very different design concept, is illustrated in two tapestries, *Moon Goddess* (Figure 6–4) and *Mother and Child* (Figure C–40 on page 79), by Wendell H. Teegarden. Both were woven on a wool warp, 8 ends per inch with a 20/2 wool weft of three to five strands. Each tapestry relies on the character of the interlocked joinings and clearly defined lines of the composition, rather than on a wealth of color. In *Mother and Child,* the centuries-old technique of weaving the vertical design horizontally on the loom is most successful. This custom, illustrated in Figures 6–4a and b, allows the vertical details of the final hanging (b) to be created with weft (a) thus giving the weaver greater control of the fine lines. In addition, the strong selvages will be used at top and bottom for support.

Newer conceptions provide a change in pace. Unusual materials and the addition of rya knots give dimension and interest to *Memsahib* and *Uno* (Figures 6–5 and 6–6). In both pieces the artist used aluminum strips woven in a linen warp. In Figure 6–5 the center area was woven separately as stuffed tubular cloth with a fringe of rya knots. Both hangings were shaped after taking them off the loom.

6–5. *Memsahib,* linen and wool hanging with aluminum strips, 29½ × 44½ × 8 inches by Cynthia Schira; photo courtesy of Marna Johnson.

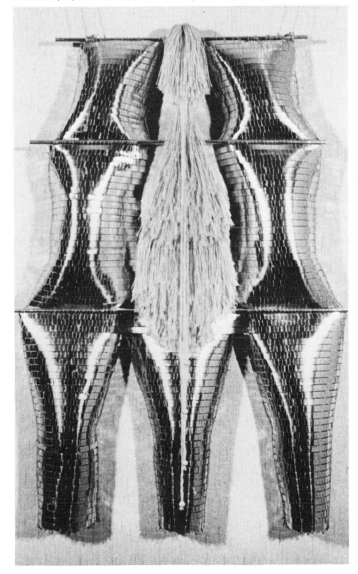

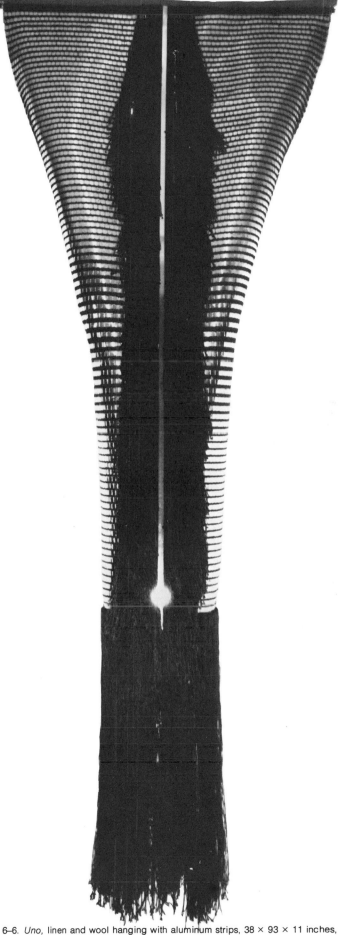

6–6. *Uno,* linen and wool hanging with aluminum strips, 38 × 93 × 11 inches, by Cynthia Schira; photo courtesy of Marna Johnson.

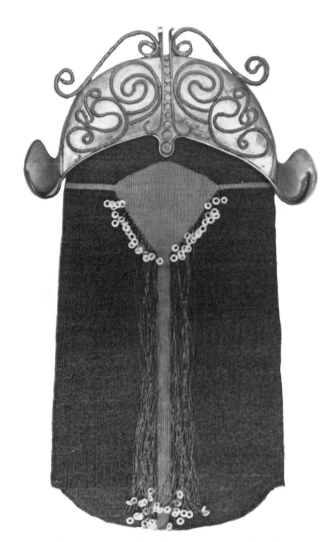

6–7. *Green Bok-Gooi*, 12 × 20 inches, wall hanging in silk, gold yarns, gold-plated brass, and bone beads by Jon Riis with metalwork by Richard Mafong; photo courtesy of the artists.

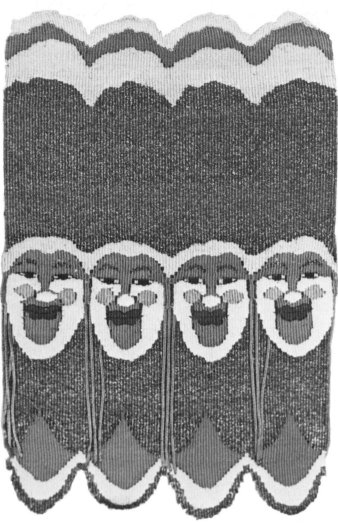

6–8. *Faces Four*, silk wall hanging, 9 × 15 inches, by Jon Riis; photo courtesy of the artist.

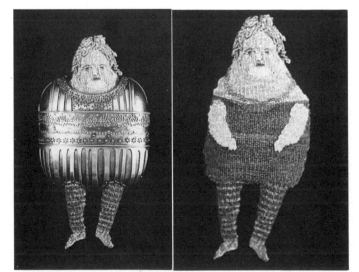

6–9. *Baby Jane*, woven figure by Jon Riis wearing metal armour by Richard Mafong; photos courtesy of the artists.

6–9a. *Baby Jane*, showing woven stuffed figure.

Fine work created by the cooperation between a weaver and a metal-worker, some of which is illustrated in Chapter 2, has resulted in a series of unified and exquisitely crafted pieces, which are further proof that work does not have to be large or overpowering to be important. These pieces are shaped on the loom, and the weaver's method of working with slits and wrapping is very effective (Figures 6–7 to 6–11).

In contrast, the tapestries in Figures 6–12 and 6–13 are of immense proportions. Jute fringes form heavy masses as a main part of the design as well as smaller accents. Strongly influenced by African masks, these vertically woven tapestries were executed with very strong color contrasts in an interlocking tapestry technique.

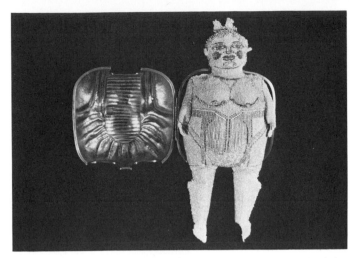

6–10. *Golden Girl* (open), woven stuffed figure by Jon Riis, metalwork by Richard Mafong; photo courtesy of the artists.

6–12. Tapestry in wool and jute by Napoleon Henderson; photo by Edward Miller.

6–13. Tapestry with wool and jute knots and fringes by Napoleon Henderson; photo by Edward Miller.

6–11. *Silesia,* metallic yarn and colored copper hanging, 9 × 30 inches by Jon Riis and Richard Mafong; photo courtesy of the artists.

6–11a. Detail.

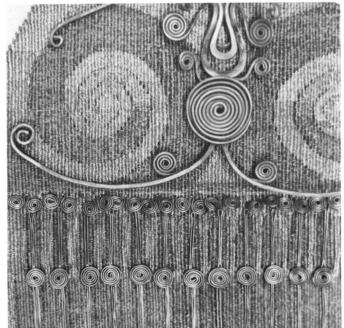

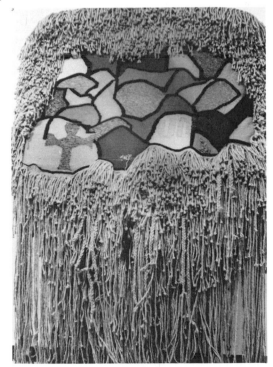

6–14. *Waterfall,* stuffed tapestry with unspun yarns by Karen Hanson; photo by Edward Miller.

6–15. *Birch Bark Eye* by Dr. Max Kaplan.

Design inspiration can come from many sources. It is surprising how representational of nature's forms a weaving can be. *Waterfall* (Figure 6–14) conveys an image simply yet powerfully, by using off-loom manipulation (after the tapestry was woven in traditional fashion) stuffing, and clever extrusion of hanks of unspun yarn. How close to nature an artist's expression can come, sometimes even unconsciously, is shown in Figures 6–15, 6–16, and 6–17. An eye specialist created a photograph of a tree trunk in *Birch Bark Eye* that has a great similarity to the two weavings, although none of the artists knew each other's work. *The Inner Eye* was woven to represent an eye, with an insertion of reflective smoky Plexiglas as well as details in rya knots and loops on a tapestry background. In Figure 6–17, the weaver created the eye image in an unconscious way, using fringes, soumak knots, and tapestry weaves in a more textured and freer interpretation.

6–16. *The Inner Eye* by Rochella Cooper; photo courtesy of the artist.

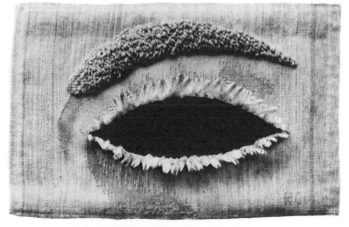

6-17. Wall hanging in tapestry, soumak, and rya techniques by Jane Redman; photo by Edward Miller.

6–18. Tapestry in Peruvian warp interlock technique by Sigrid Weltge; photo courtesy of the artist.

6–18a. Diagram of tapestry warp, showing the start of three areas of weft.

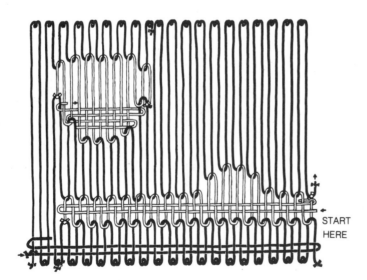

START
HERE

Peruvian warp interlock technique

Giving the appearance of a tapestry weave, the black-and-white hanging in Figure 6–18 illustrates the use of a technique that gives ultimate scope for expanses of pure color and richly textured areas. In this technique, the warp and weft yarns can be the same, and are interlocked with each other in a 50-50 plain-weave structure. Unlike a traditional weft-faced tapestry, which has many more wefts than warps, this uses an equal number of threads of the same yarn in both weft and warp. The structure is very different from what we normally call tapestry. The weaving is best done on a frame, which remains as part of the piece for hanging.

The planned design is first drawn full-scale on paper and taped to the back of the frame (Figure 6–18a). The colors of looping then follow the outline of the cartoon. Here, there are two colors, black and white. The warp is started by tying the first warp thread to the frame, as shown on the drawing. The next color is interlooped and is tied to the third color. The looping continues up and down the frame in continuous motion.

When the warp is finished in this way, the design is already completed, and the hanging could be left without weaving. In the work shown here, however, the weft was woven through on butterflies. At the points where warp and weft are wound to the frame, the yarn has to be wrapped around the frame twice in order to cover the frame as well as to prevent slippage of the threads. In the weaving of the white circle there has to be an occasional slit to make up for the length of the black side thread—it is only interlocked every second or third row. Many variations are possible once the weaver experiments with this excitingly new old technique.

Combined techniques

The small detail in Figure 6–19 shows clearly how textures can be used for their own sake. The play between the flat areas, stripes, and rows of chaining, soumak, and looped and fringed rya knots make an unpretentious, direct design that relies very much on the arrangement of proportions between the areas.

When craftsmanship is paired with great imaginative force the result is exciting. Spurning the well-known devices of surface enhancement by simple insertion of knots, the weaver of Figure 6–20 has created woven bands and wrapped tubes that give the effect of snaking out of the woven background. Perfect curving of the slits, the understatement of color, and the excellent proportion of heavy and lightweight areas make this hanging a notable design. Relying more on color, the hanging in Figure 6–21 by the same weaver demands interest because of the on-loom shaping that converts a rectangle into a freer but unified form.

6–19. Detail of weaving by Janice Mouton, showing texture combinations created by rya, chaining, soumak, and loop techniques.

6–21. Wall hanging by Astra Kleinhofs-Strobel; photo courtesy of the artist.

6–20. Large wall hanging by Astra Kleinhofs-Strobel; photo courtesy of the artist.

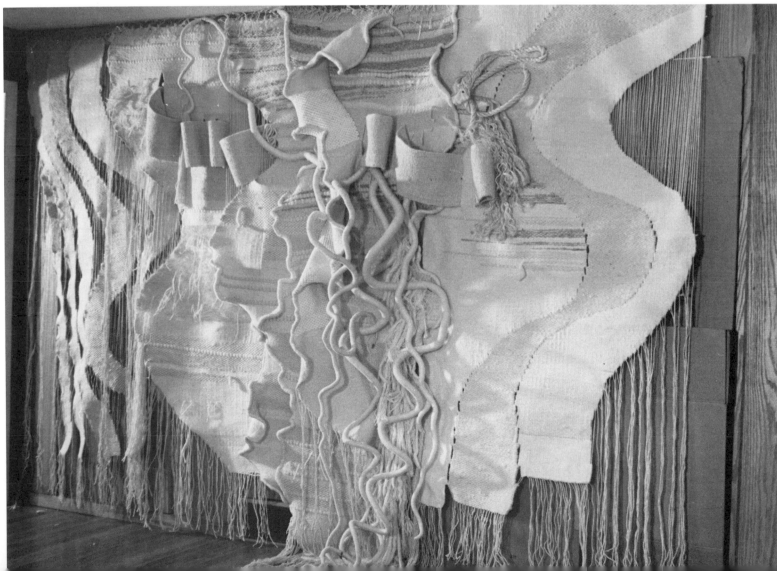

6–22. *Delicate Flight,* hanging in jute and handspun wool, with fringe of Persian rug knots, 96 × 84 inches, by Dorothy A. Hughes; photo courtesy of the artist.

6–22a. Detail.

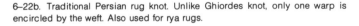

6–22b. Traditional Persian rug knot. Unlike Ghiordes knot, only one warp is encircled by the weft. Also used for rya rugs.

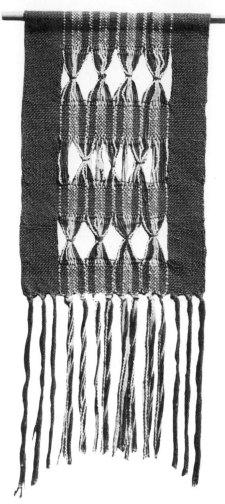

6–23. Small open-weave hanging by Else Regensteiner, used as sample; photo by John W. Rosenthal.

The large tapestry (8×7 feet) by Dorothy Hughes was woven on a linen warp with her own handspun jute weft together with flax and hemp (Figure 6–22). The rya fringe, which is a large part of the design, is made in Persian rug knots (Figure 6–22b).

No matter what the weave, prototypes are sometimes useful for developing ideas before large pieces are made. Figures 6–23 and 6–24 show prototypes for open weaves. In one, the warp was left open and later grouped and tied; in the other, Brooks Bouquet technique was worked on an open shed, as shown in the drawing 6–24a. A manipulated flat hanging, that is, one not used the way it is woven, is shown in Figure 6–26. The warp is shaded from yellow through orange, with dark bands at two sides. These colors are repeated in the weft. Woven on the loom as a rectangle, dowels are included in the weaving by, first, looping the warp around one stick attached to the warp beam and, second, setting the other stick parallel to one side of the warp and including it with the weft shuttle in every other pick. Parallel to the other side of the warp, an extra thread is set in the same way, to make a weft fringe. This hanging uses an M & O threading, but other patterns would also be attractive. A wooden tinker-toy disk holds the dowels so that the rectangular shape is transformed into a diamond or rhomb when the weaving is off the loom.

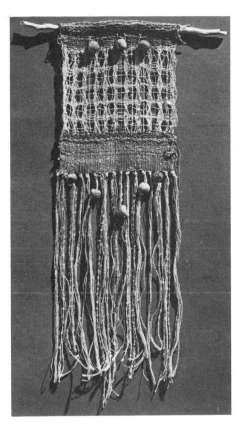

6–24. Miniature hanging using Brooks Bouquet, by Else Regensteiner; photo by John W. Rosenthal.

6–24a. The technique of Brooks Bouquet on an open shed.

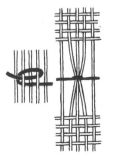

6–25. *Madam Butterfly*, miniature hanging with supplementary warp, by Betty Jo Tricou.

6–26. Hanging with tinker toy, woven as a *rectangle* on the loom with supports for hanging as *diamond* shape, by Lou Olson.

6–26a. Diagram.

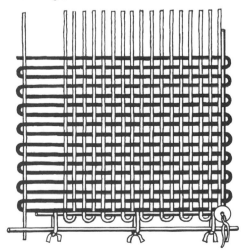

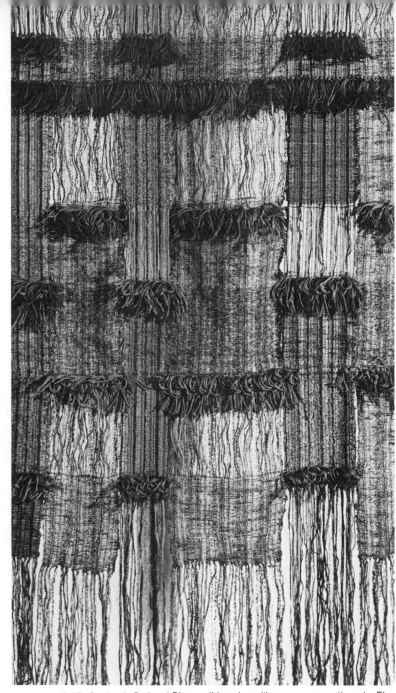

6–28. *Woodland,* hanging in natural wools with inserts of bark, by Else Regensteiner; photo by John W. Rosenthal.

6–27. *Design in Red and Blue,* wall hanging with open warp sections, by Else Regensteiner. Also shown in color on page 76 (Figure C–29).

6–29. Decorative mat with inlaid H. V. design, from Finland.

PLAIN WEAVES

Plain weaves can be used for wall hangings and enhanced with many different techniques. When the color of the warp is vivid, the warp can be left open as a design factor, as shown in Figure 6–27. Natural materials can be effective in a plain-weave hanging when they are integrally related to the character of the fabric. In order to support the bark, stone, or other natural object on the surface, a backing must be woven behind it. Unspun wools and natural yarns are particularly congenial to such design conceptions (Figure 6–28).

Plain weave is also used effectively in a lovely, well-controlled design from Finland (Figure 6–29), in which laid-in threads create the pattern on top of the basic plain-weave structure. This is called the H. V. technique, from the Swedish word for half tapestry, *Halvgobelang.* The small hanging called *Spaceship Earth* (Figure 6–30) shows a different approach to this supplementary weft technique. Unspun wool and novelty yarn were laid in on a blue background, and beads were used to enrich the top and fringe, helping to make them as much a part of the piece as the central design.

6–30. *Spaceship Earth,* small hanging in laid-in technique by Betty Jo Tricou.

The Meet-and-Separate technique

A plain-weave technique which closely resembles the hatching method of tapestry (Figure 6–33) is what weaver Peter Collingwood calls "Meet and Separate," a method of changing color across a row by starting two different threads from each selvage and then turning each one back, using either the slit or interlock joining (See Figures 6–2a–d). The technique can give three areas: two separate blocks of color and one shaded block created by a combination of the two colors. Figures 6–31 and 6–32 show pleasingly geometrical hangings based on this use of plain weave.

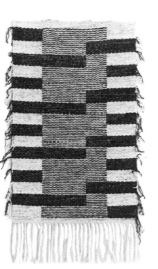

6–31. Hanging in Meet-and-Separate technique by Sandra Ullman; photo courtesy of the artist.

6–32. Large hanging in Meet-and-Separate technique by Jane K. Busse; photo courtesy of the artist.

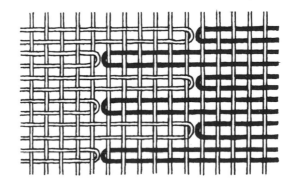

6–33. Diagram for the Meet-and-Separate technique.

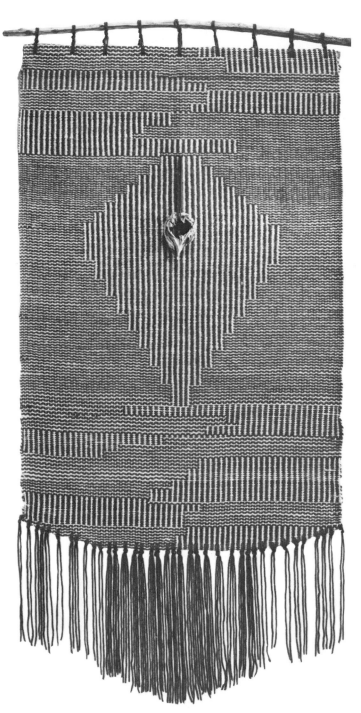

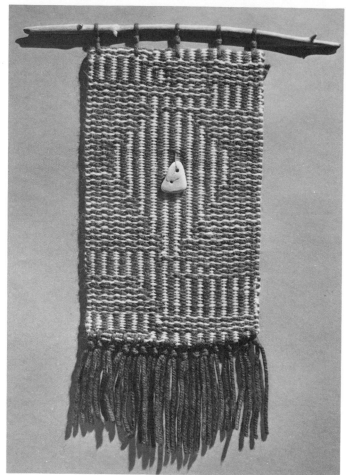

6–35. Prototype for *Wooden Image* by Else Regensteiner; photo by John W. Rosenthal. The center of each design carries out the shapes of the driftwood and stone, which provide the motifs of the hangings.

The Crossed-Wefts technique

Another technique worked out by Peter Collingwood, which he calls "Crossed-Wefts" and uses for rugs, also can be effectively used in wall hangings, as shown in Figures 6–34 and 6–35. This technique results in designs made by alternating two colors in the weft. There are many methods of crossed-weft weaving, which give many design variations. Details are given for two of them. In order to make the following directions visually clear, I am calling the two colors "light" and "dark." Horizontal and vertical lines give the appearance of tapestry but in reality the fabric is woven from selvage to selvage, and the lines are made by changing the alternation of colors by crossing them at pre-determined points, A and B. The design is clearest when woven in heavy yarns on a widely spaced cotton or linen warp, approximately 5 or 6 ends per inch. The threading is on harnesses 1, 2, 3 and 4, but it can also be done on two harnesses.

Method I: center design of vertical lines framed by side areas of horizontal lines.

(1) Determine two crossing points where horizontal and vertical lines will interchange. The left crossing point is here called A, the right crossing is called B.

(2) For A, the first (left) crossing: Begin weaving from left

6–34. *Wooden Image*, wall hanging in Crossed-Weft technique by Else Regensteiner, photo by John W. Rosenthal.

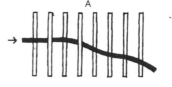

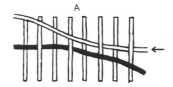

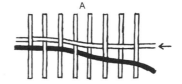

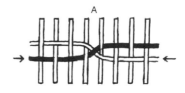

selvage. Raise harnesses 1 and 3. Insert dark shuttle from left selvage to point A. Bring dark shuttle out of the shed at point A and set it down. With harnesses 1 and 3 still raised, now insert light shuttle from right selvage to point A. Bring shuttle out of the shed at point A but keep holding it. (Note that the warp between the two weft threads is in the down position.)

(3) Change shed to harnesses 2 and 4. The center thread between the wefts is now up. Pass the light shuttle over this thread into the shed and over to the left selvage. This makes the light thread pass over two threads at this pick.

(4) With harnesses 2 and 4 still raised, pick up the dark shuttle, cross over the light thread at point A and insert the shuttle *straight up* into the shed so that it does not pass over two warps. Continue to right selvage. This completes a crossing at A.

(5) For B, the second (right) crossing: Change shed to 1 and 3. Insert dark shuttle from the right selvage to point B. Bring shuttle out of shed at B and put it down. Insert light shuttle from left selvage and bring it out at point B (the warp thread between the wefts is down).

(6) Change shed to 2 and 4 (warp between the wefts is now up). Pass light shuttle over the center thread and insert into shed, thereby passing over two warp threads at this pick. Pass shuttle through to right selvage.

(7) With harnesses 2 and 4 still raised, insert dark shuttle into shed at B, crossing the light thread so that it does *not* pass over the two warps, and continue to left selvage. This completes the crossing at B.

These steps are repeated and the crossing points changed according to the design. Note that the order of crossing the shuttles can be reversed so that either color can cross over the other.

Method II: horizontal lines in center, framed by vertical lines. In this technique both colors start from the same selvage.

(1) Raise harnesses 1 and 3. Pass light shuttle from left to right selvage.

(2) Change shed to 2 and 4. Pass dark shuttle from left to right selvage.

(3) Change shed to 1 and 3. Pass light shuttle from right to point B.

(4) Change shed to 2 and 4. Pass dark shuttle from right to point B.

(5) Change shed to 1 and 3. Pass the dark shuttle over the left raised warp and under the next into the shed and across to point A.

(6) Change shed to 2 and 4. Pass light shuttle across the dark weft into the shed and across to point A.

(7) Change shed to 1 and 3. Pass light shuttle into shed at A and over to left selvage.

(8) Change shed to 2 and 4. Pass dark shuttle over light weft and into the shed to left selvage. Continue these eight steps, changing design as desired.

6–36. Crossed-Weft technique, Method I. This shows the first steps in crossing warp at point A.

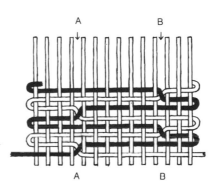

6–36a. Crossed-Weft technique, Method I. The crossings at both A and B are shown. The color change in the crossed wefts produces a vertical design in center of the weaving.

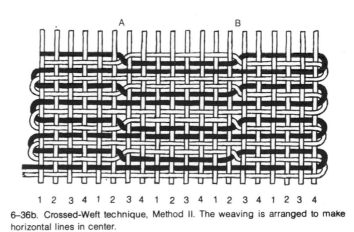

1 2 3 4 1 2 3 4 1 2 3 4 1 2 3 4 1 2 3 4

6–36b. Crossed-Weft technique, Method II. The weaving is arranged to make horizontal lines in center.

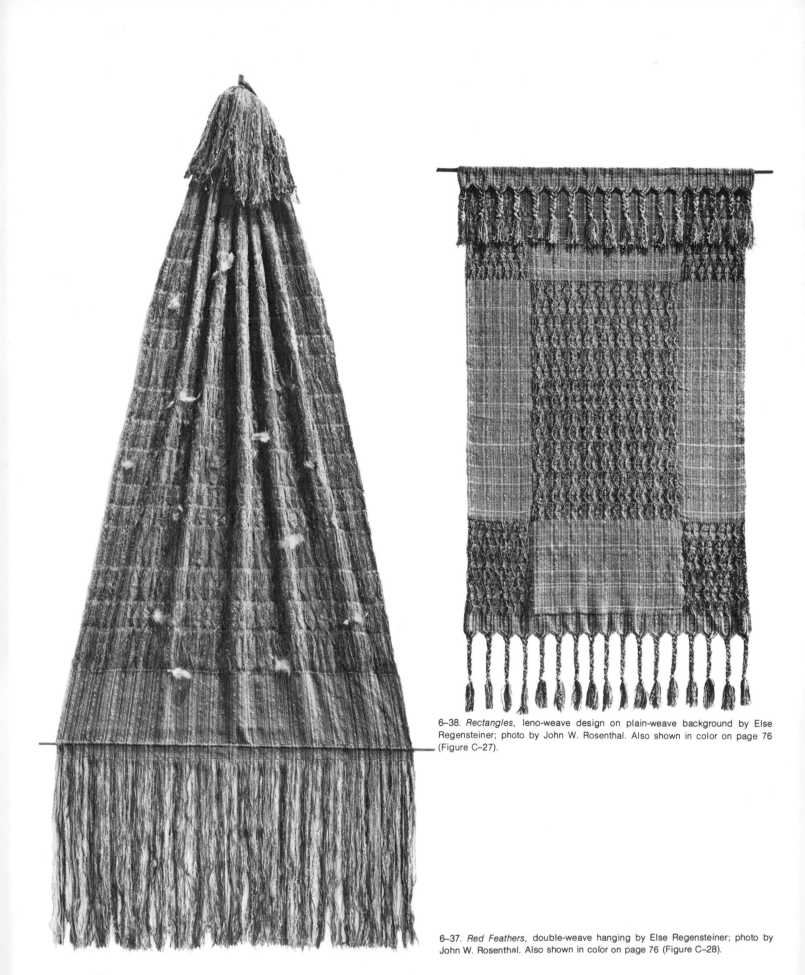

6–38. *Rectangles*, leno-weave design on plain-weave background by Else Regensteiner; photo by John W. Rosenthal. Also shown in color on page 76 (Figure C–27).

6–37. *Red Feathers*, double-weave hanging by Else Regensteiner; photo by John W. Rosenthal. Also shown in color on page 76 (Figure C–28).

DOUBLE WEAVES

Double weaves appear in all forms in wall hangings and are a great favorite of artists because of their three-dimensional impact. The double weaves illustrated in Figures 6–37 and 6–38 and elsewhere in the book range from tubular hangings to multiple-layer weaves in which there are great possibilities for technical variations. The colors can be manipulated in various ways, such as having the top layer a lace-type weave through which the background shows, or having the two layers interchangeable, which is especially apparent in the traditional pick-up method of double weave.

Double weave with pick-up design

As in all traditional double-weave methods, the warp must be planned for two layers of fabric to be woven simultaneously on top of each other (twice as many warp threads as for one layer). The warp is set up in the usual manner, but the colors for each layer are different in order to bring out the design, which is in contrasting colors as shown in color on page 75 (Figure C–25). In these examples the warp is threaded in the harnesses as follows:

harness 1—light thread
harness 2—dark thread
harness 3—light thread
harness 4—dark thread

One light and one dark thread are sleyed through the same dent. In this method, harnesses 1 and 3 carry the threads for the light layer; harnesses 2 and 4 carry the threads for the dark layer.

The pattern should be worked out on graph paper, with filled-in squares representing the design. The design appears in the reverse color on the reverse of the fabric; that is, if the design is dark on a light background on the right side, it will be light on a dark background on the reverse. Two shuttles, one wound with each color, and a pick-up stick are needed. The pick-up stick should be longer than the width of the warp and about one-inch high. The weaving procedure is as follows:

(1) Raise harnesses 2 and 4 (dark warp); with the beater at rest position (away from you), slide the point of the pick-up stick over and under the dark warp threads, picking up all design threads indicated in the first (bottom) row of the graph-paper plan. This will give you the dark design on the light background. When the stick is inserted for the full width of the warp, slide it (with it's picked-up threads) back against the reed, letting it ride on top of the shed. Release treadles.

(2) Treadle harness 1 which raises the first half of the light layer. Weave with light weft. Beat without removing the stick. Slide stick back against the reed again. Release treadle.

(3) Treadle harness 3 to raise the other half of the light warp. Weave light. Take out the pick-up stick and beat. Be sure to always leave a wide arc of weft in the shed, to assure good edges.

(4) Treadle 1 and 3 (all light warp threads). With the stick, pick up the background threads which were just woven, as

6–39. *Trees,* pick-up double weave by Dorothy Novotny; photo by Edward Miller.

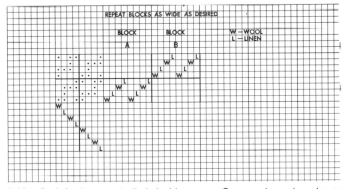

6–39a. Draft for loom-controlled double weave, *Games,* shown in color on page 75 (Figure C–25). Two warp beams are used, the first with 8/3 Swedish linen, and the second, which is woven with lighter tension, with dark red wool and cowhair. The weft is in various rug and tapestry yarns. The six-dent reed is sleyed with one linen and one wool end per dent.

indicated in the graph, again working from right to left. Release treadles.

(5) Treadle harness 2, and weave with the dark weft. Beat as well as possible with the stick in position. Slide stick against the reed. Release treadle.

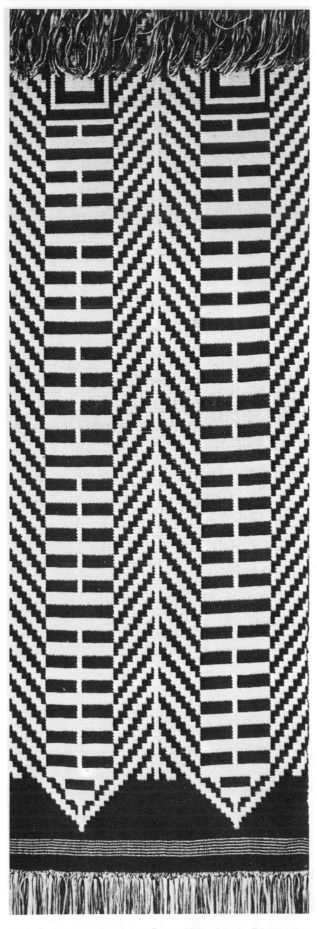

6–40. Double-weave hanging by Roanne Katz; photo by Edward Miller.

(6) Treadle harness 4, and weave dark. Remove pick-up stick and beat. This completes one set of pick-up. If the woven design does not make a square with two picks in each layer for each row of the graph, use as many sets of the same picks as necessary to complete the proper proportions.

This method of weaving a reversible double-weave design is simpler than it may appear. Once the process is understood, it can be summarized this way:

(1) Raise harnesses 2 and 4 (pick up pattern—dark warp).
(2) Raise harness 1 (weave light).
(3) Raise harness 3 (weave light).
(4) Raise harness 1 and 3 (pick up background—light warp).
(5) Raise harness 2 (weave dark).
(6) Raise harness 4 (weave dark).

It must be noted that the warp as well as the weft can be composed of many colors, as long as the colors in one layer make a pleasing contrast with the other layer. For other variations of double weave see *The Art of Weaving,* Chapter 6.

Tubular weaves

As discussed in Chapter 2; the easiest tubular weave requires only one shuttle, which goes around and around from the top layer to the bottom and back. The stuffing is often commercial polyester or yarn remnants, cottons, or whatever is on hand. The warp for tubular weave must consist of an odd number of threads, to prevent adjacent threads at the edges from being woven alike. As in most double weaves, the number of ends per inch must be doubled, since there are two layers, and must be sleyed two per dent.

PATTERN WEAVES

We are so used to seeing traditional pattern weaves in coverlets and furnishings that it is refreshing to find that they can be included very attractively in a wall hanging. The flowerlike design in Figure 6–41 was picked up in dark blue, with touches of yellow, using the traditional tapestry joining. The background is in two shades of white, the lighter used as tabby, and gives a shadowed effect. The tabby is the same for design and background. Figure 6–41b is the draft for only the upper flower section, as the stem section is not a repeat pattern.

The conjunction of the artist's vision and the weaver's understanding of structures is demonstrated most vividly in the Op-Art hanging *Circus Op* (Figure 6–43). The optical illusion of moving areas and lines, and the appearance of three-dimensional space and depth is achieved solely by the proportioning of the size of blocks in weft as well as warp. Color

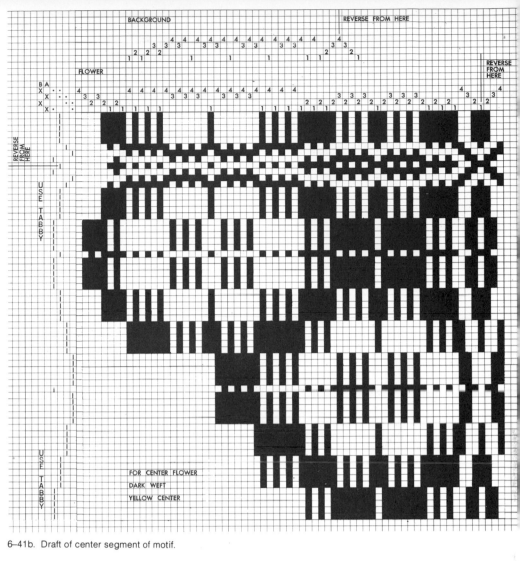

6–41b. Draft of center segment of motif.

6–42. Pattern weave with tapestry and fringe by Stana Coleman; photo by Robert Fields.

6–41. *Blue Clover*, wall hanging, 44 × 00 inches, in pattern weave by Alice Eckley; photo by Robert Fields.

6–41a. Detail.

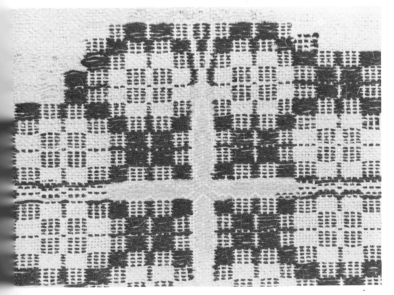

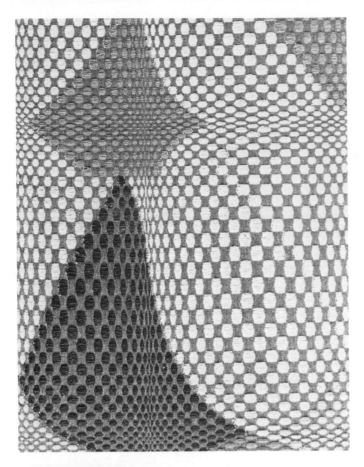

changes inserted in tapestry-like fashion emphasize the illusion of approaching and receding forms. The two drafts for this six-harness design explain the threading, arrangement of the blocks, and treadling. Proportioning blocks from wide to narrow, and reverse, can be applied to many other threadings, such as Summer and Winter, with similarly interesting results.

6–43. Detail of *Circus Op* by Laurie Herrick; photo by Anne Dengler. The full piece is shown in color on page 79 (Figure C–38).

6–43a. Closer detail.

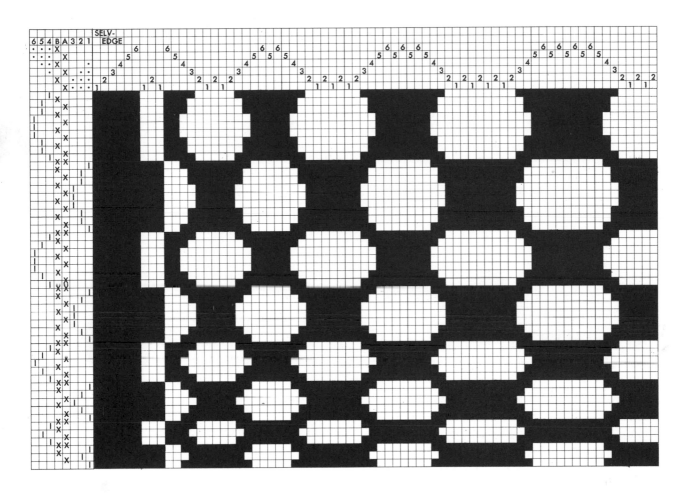

6–43b. Draft. Tabby is used alternately on pattern; both A and B are used between blocks. Read draft from bottom upward. See 6–43c for the complete threading and treadling sequence.

6–43c. Threading. Tabby is used alternately within blocks; both A and B are used at the end of each block. For wider blocks, increase number of 5–6 and 1–2 threading to required width. Threading is shown on two lines but should be read continuously left to right.

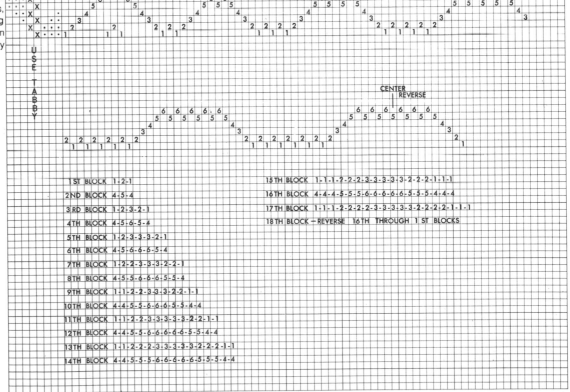

1ST BLOCK 1-2-1	15TH BLOCK 1-1-1-2-2-2-3-3-3-3-3-2-2-2-1-1-1
2ND BLOCK 4-5-4	16TH BLOCK 4-4-4-5-5-5-6-6-6-6-6-5-5-5-4-4-4
3RD BLOCK 1-2-3-2-1	17TH BLOCK 1-1-1-2-2-2-2-3-3-3-3-3-2-2-2-2-1-1-1
4TH BLOCK 4-5-6-5-4	18TH BLOCK — REVERSE 16TH THROUGH 1 ST BLOCKS
5TH BLOCK 1-2-3-3-2-1	
6TH BLOCK 4-5-6-6-5-4	
7TH BLOCK 1-2-2-3-3-3-2-2-1	
8TH BLOCK 4-5-5-6-6-6-5-5-4	
9TH BLOCK 1-1-2-2-3-3-3-2-2-1-1	
10TH BLOCK 4-4-5-5-6-6-6-5-5-4-4	
11TH BLOCK 1-1-2-2-3-3-3-3-3-2-2-1-1	
12TH BLOCK 4-4-5-5-6-6-6-6-6-5-5-4-4	
13TH BLOCK 1-1-2-2-2-3-3-3-3-3-2-2-2-1-1	
14TH BLOCK 4-4-5-5-5-6-6-6-6-6-5-5-5-4-4	

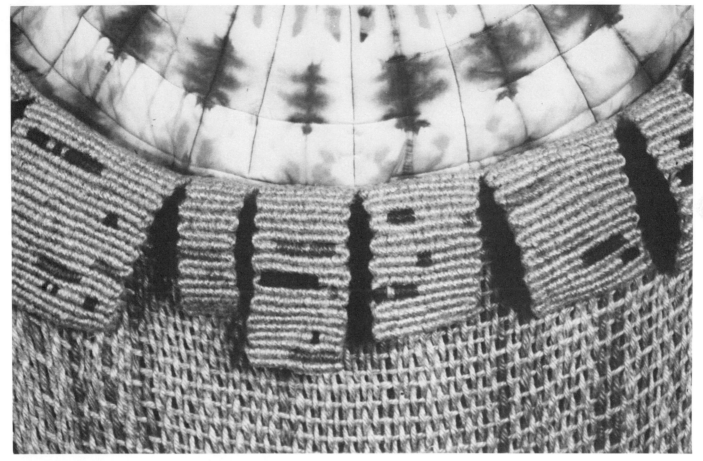

6–44a. Detail.

6–44. Three-dimensional wall piece in combined techniques by Michi Ouchi; photo courtesy of the artist.

TIE DYEING

Tie-dyeing has been explored by handweavers for many purposes. In wall hangings the technique can be used to show designs made in "resist" technique by tying sections of the warp or weft according to the design and dyeing the untied parts. When untied, the design will show in natural color against the dyed background. Yarns can be dyed in any commercial or natural dyebath which is appropriate to the fibers being used, to create designs from either the dyed or undyed portions of the yarn.

In a freer manner, warps can be painted right on the loom and woven either in plain or tapestry fashion, as shown in color on page 79 (Figure C–39). Even the woven fabric can be used as a canvas and painted during the weaving process; in this way, areas of painting and tapestry can be combined for an interesting play of textures.

Tie-dyed strips of cloth were cleverly interwoven with cotton and wool in *Woven Brocade,* shown in color on page 77 (Figure C–32). Woven sideways on the loom, the piece shows understanding and a strong and expressive handling of an intricate technique. How congenial combinations of techniques and materials can be is shown in Figure 6–44, where tie-dyed fabric, macramé, and weaving have been combined in a three-dimensional hanging.

Warp dyeing

In more intricate designs, the warp can be dyed in several colors in the following manner (directions kindly supplied by Fran Weintraub Lasky):

6–45. Tie-dyed warp woven with dowels by Fran Weintraub Lasky; photo courtesy of the artist.

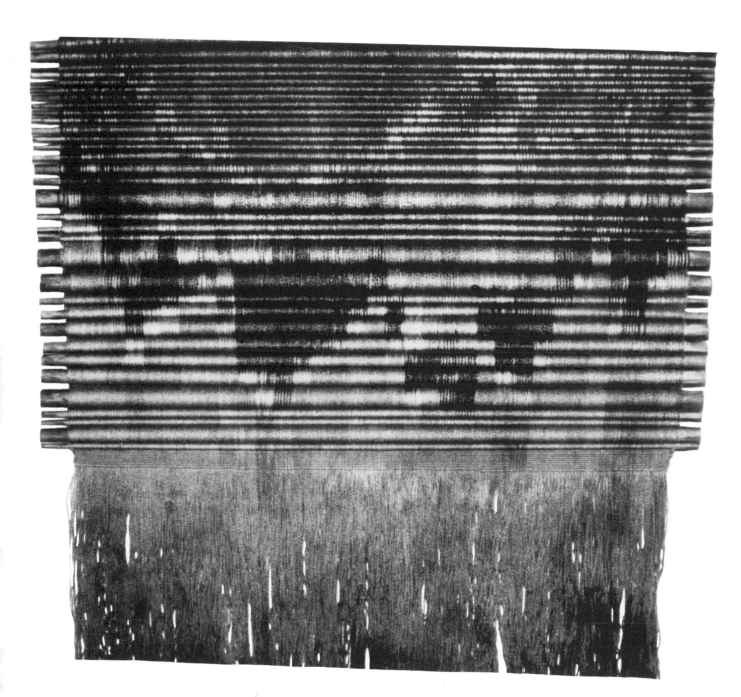

6–46. Wall hanging with tie-dyed warp and stitchery, 24 × 36 inches, by Fran Weintraub Lasky; photo courtesy of the artist.

Work out a plan of the several color areas, and determine how many warp ends will be used in each area. Then wind the warp on the board, bundling together the number of ends required for each one-inch width. Secure the cross with a longer string than usual before removing the warp from the board. Remove the warp without cutting the loops. Slip a wooden rod through the loops and lay the warp on the floor or table. Separate the one-inch bundles with a spreader.

With masking tape, tightly bind the two sides of the first area to be dyed. This prevents the dye from bleeding outside the planned area. Then bundle the warp so that every area is bound except the section to be dyed, which should be loose. Dunk this loose area into the dyebath for as long as needed. At the same time, dye a skein of the weft yarn for weaving with the same color.

Each dyed area must have thoroughly dried before the warp can be retied for the next stage of dyeing. Note that the first dyeing should be the lightest color, and each successive dyeing the next darker color.

The tie-dyed warp is put on the loom in the regular way and can be woven in weaves which show up the dyed warp areas as the principal design factor, as shown in color on page 77 (Figure C–30), or with weft yarns flowing across the warp areas so that colors overlap and interact. A detail of a tie-dyed warp woven with various dowels gives a warp-faced effect (See Figure 6–45). There are many ways an imaginative weaver can take advantage of tie-dyed warps in conjunction with rya knots, laid-in wefts, tapestry technique, and so forth.

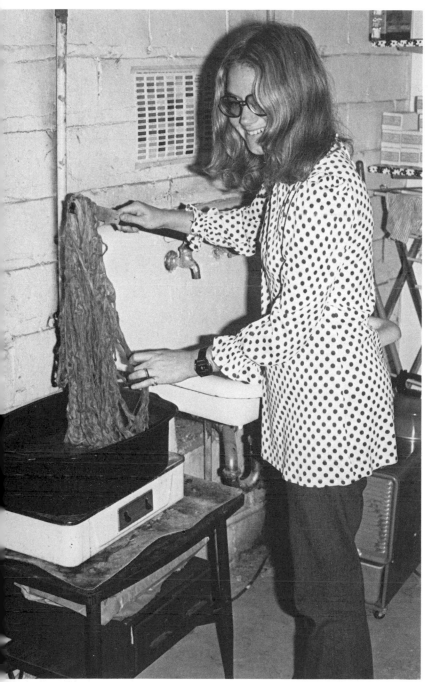

6–47. Skeins in the dye pot; all photos of technique courtesy of Fran Weintraub Lasky.

6–47a. Partially taped warp in the dye pot.

6–47b. Warp spread out to show arrangements of dyed parts.

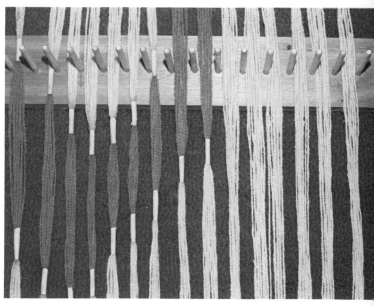

6–48. Design for weaving with tie-dyed weft, by Lynda Y. Cannon; photos of all techniques and pieces courtesy of the artist.

6–48a. Weft tied for dyeing the bird design.

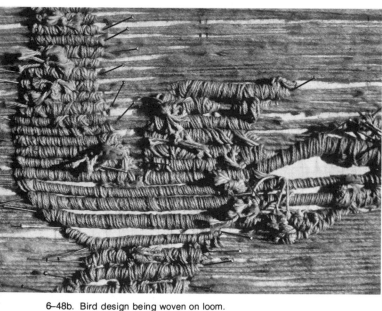

6–48b. Bird design being woven on loom.

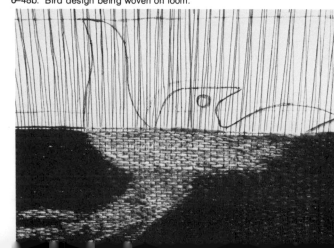

Weft dyeing

The weft, too, can be tie-dyed for interesting design manipulation. Directions for resist dyeing the weft, so that the weft pattern will show against the dyed area, are as follows (kindly supplied by Lynda Y. Cannon and Lydia Van Gelder, who developed the technique).

Use a wooden two-by-four board for winding the weft. It should be approximately 6 inches longer than the width the weaving will be; this allowance will be taken up in the design for the weaving. Hammer nails, around which the weft will be wound, into the board near each end, and tape brown wrapping paper around the width between the nails. The width of the weaving is indicated on the paper, and also the areas to be tied, as shown in Figure 6–49a.

Now tie the weft to one nail and wind back and forth around the nails to the amount needed for the piece (Figure 6–49b). If a large piece is planned, this process may require two or more duplicate skeining boards. The duplication also allows pattern variations to be created.

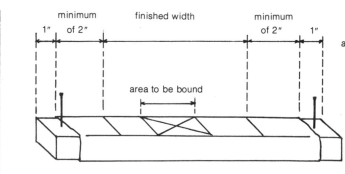

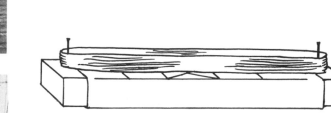

6–49. Steps in weft-resist dyeing, by Lynda Y. Cannon. (a) board for winding the weft; (b) winding the weft; (c) binding the wound weft previous to dyeing; (d) binding completed.

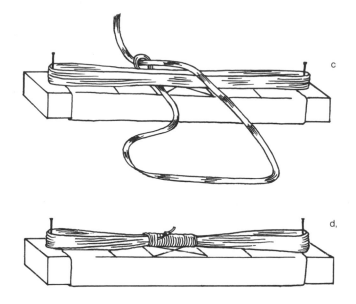

c

d,

Another way of achieving a tie-dyed design in the weft is to lay the weft across a drawing made in the exact size of the woven piece, pinning the weft down on the drawing and tightly wrapping the enclosed weft area to protect it from the dyebath. When this dyed weft is woven, the pattern appears in the undyed area. In the bird design illustrating this method (See Figure 6–48), a handspun wool was used on a fine wool warp, which adds to the soft-edged effect this technique can achieve.

Wrap tightly the area on the skein which corresponds to the design area marked on the brown paper. To facilitate binding, several strands of wrapping cords could be doubled over and fastened by a slip knot around the skein (Figures 6–49c and d). When the design area has been protected by the wrapping, the skein is ready to be dyed, dried, washed, and woven. In weaving with this weft, which is wound on a shuttle, the color areas are placed according to each line of the design (Figure 6–50a). This results in uneven edges, which take up the allowance made previously in the winding of the skeins. The loopy edges can all be cut the same length for fringe on the sides or they can be turned under and stitched for framing the piece.

6–50. Tie-dyed weft design by Lynda Y. Cannon.

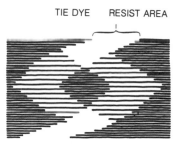

TIE DYE   RESIST AREA

6–50a. Design for Figure 6–50, with each line representing the placement of the resist area of each consecutive pick.

6–51. *Lacy Tree,* by Linda Howard; photo by Edward Miller.

6–52. Large wall hanging with stuffed tubes by Joyce Richards; photo by Robert Fields.

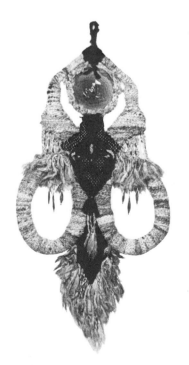

6–53. Wall hanging inspired by Chilkat blanket, by Ann Bernard Boone; photo courtesy of the artist.

SCULPTURAL HANGINGS

It is obvious that contemporary weavers are extensively exploring the possibilities of sculptural shaping of wall hangings. Dropping warp threads at the sides and later cutting them off produces the tree-like shape in Figure 6–51. In a loose open-weave hanging like this, inserted rods are necessary to provide support and shaping.

Stuffing is another way to provide shaping in three-dimensional pieces. Stuffed tubes are effectively combined with areas of other techniques in the hanging in Figure 6–52, which is organized into a unity by the well-defined shaping of the final piece. The shaped wall hanging in Figure 6–53 was inspired by a Chilkat blanket from the American Indians of the Northwest Coast. Many techniques are coordinated, including proportional arrangement of the elements, striking integration of the fringe, and careful shaping and finishing of the parts, which were woven separately. This piece is especially beautiful because of its natural colors in handspun wools, goat's hair, and unspun, laid-in fleece. Off-loom shaping is illustrated by *Grass Roots,* (Figure 6–55), in which tubes of hand-dyed wool and synthetics are assembled and combined by rya knots. The flexibility of the tubes gives the viewer freedom to play with the arrangement in many different arrays.

The free-standing structure in Figure 6–56 makes its own loom, with the weaving done back and forth on the frame of the structure. The frame is wood, with black leather lacing and red and white cotton cord.

6–54. *Bank Hanging,* by Ann Bernard Boone; photo courtesy of the artist.

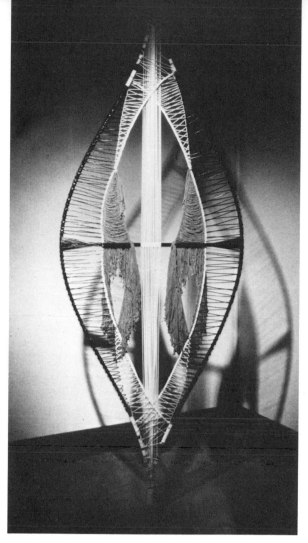

6–55. *Black, White and Red,* free-standing structure, 108 × 36 inches, by Lorraine Gonzalez; photo courtesy of Dr. Richard Gonzalez.

6–56. *Grass Roots,* tubular weave in hand-dyed wools and synthetics, 72 × 132 × 5 inches, by Jean Stamsta; photo courtesy of the artist.

6–57. *Gracilis,* standing form, three interchangeable segments of knotless netting in polypropylene monofilament, 120 inches high, by Barbara Shawcroft; photos courtesy of the artist.

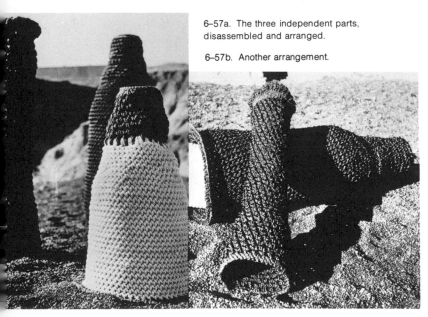

6–57a. The three independent parts, disassembled and arranged.

6–57b. Another arrangement.

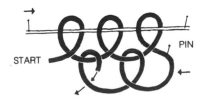

START   PIN

6–57c. The technique of knotless netting.

Off-loom techniques

There are so many books which treat off-loom techniques individually and in depth that here I would like only to show how interesting textiles can be developed by using imagination and sensitivity for design. In some of these illustrations heavy fringes and knotted jute were used along with weaving, and built into structures that are visually powerful and elegant in conception. Although there are untold variations of these and related techniques, a basic understanding of the most fundamental ones should be sufficient to encourage and stimulate exploration. The textile artist will discover that the possibilities include, just as in knotting techniques, flat and three-dimensional structures.

The intriguing standing columns by Barbara Shawcroft are made in segments which can be ordered in different arrangements, as Figure 6–57, 6–57a and 6–57b illustrate. They were created by the off-loom technique of knotless netting, which is found in many Neolithic Swiss and Pre-Columbian Peruvian textiles. It works best when fairly heavy material, such as jute, hemp, linen, or synthetics are used. Figure 6–57c shows the basic path that the continuous thread follows to interlock the rows of loops. This can form either a loose, or when pulled tightly, a dense, stiff fabric.

Generally, all work which is not designed solely for function originates in and expresses a visionary idea of the artist. For instance, in *Fourteen Stations of the Cross,* (Figure 6–61) the form was taken from the feeling of totem structures, and its design incorporated a purely visual contrast between circular shapes with a flat elongated background with the visionary

6–58. *Stucco's Passage,* three-dimensional structure of natural jute rope in knotting, loop, and stitching techniques, 36 × 24 × 24 inches, by Leora K. Stewart.

6–60. *Box Form,* sculptural hanging of knotted jute and wrapped black and white wool, 36 × 36 × 12 inches, by Leora K. Stewart; collection of Diane Kelder.

6–61. *Fourteen Stations of the Cross,* suspended piece in knotted, hand-dyed red jute, 121 × 12 × 6 inches, by Leora K. Stewart.

6–59. *Vicuna Ladder,* suspended piece (from ceiling to floor) in knotted and wrapped natural jute and black wool, 13 feet high × 2 feet wide, by Leora K. Stewart.

idea. Stones with holes worn by the power of the lake were the inspiration for *Sandpiper* and *Dancing Stones,* and driftwood and fishermen's nets suggested *The Nets are Empty,* which combines a woven background with knotting in wool, jute and horsehair (Figures 6–63, 6–64, and 6–65). In *Guards* (Figure 6–69) two monumental columns tower over the human figure. Each is obviously woven in two pieces. They illustrate how important sculptural pieces can be, even when woven with utmost limitation of tools and techniques, if they are handled with skill and a good sense of proportion and design. The loom-shaped hanging by the same artist *Medicine Man,* (Figure 6–68) also over eight feet high, is equally as powerful. Its handspun yarns bring out the best in the artist's understated approach.

In textile art, as in abstract painting, it is intriguing to try to penetrate into the artist's mind to reach the conception behind his finished piece. Textile art provides the artist-weaver a great range of variables to work out his ideas. Not only color, shape, and form, but the whole play of textures are added to the visual impact. I hope the examples provided will encourage many weavers to extend the outer boundaries of our craft.

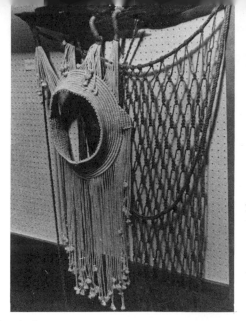

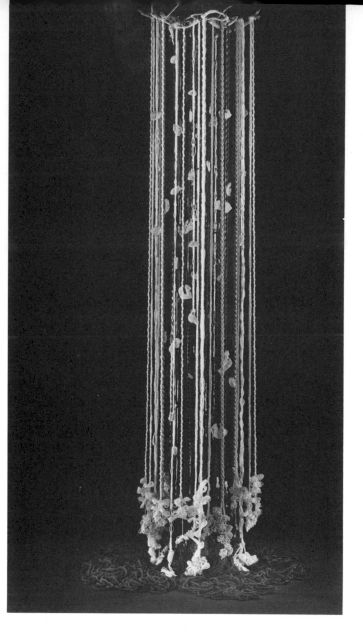

6–62. *The Ghost of Captain Seavey,* hanging in macramé and knotting by E. C. Helfrich, photo by J. W. Howlett.

6–63. *Sandpiper,* hanging by Else Regensteiner; photo by John W. Rosenthal.

6–64. *Dancing Stones,* woven and knotted structure embellished with stones that have natural holes in them, by Else Regensteiner; photo by John W. Rosenthal.

6–64a. Detail.

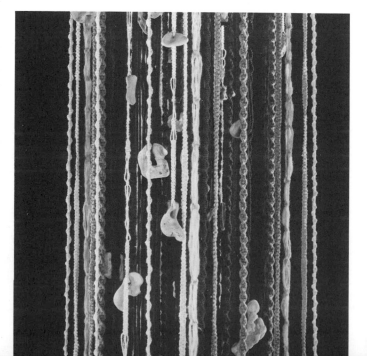

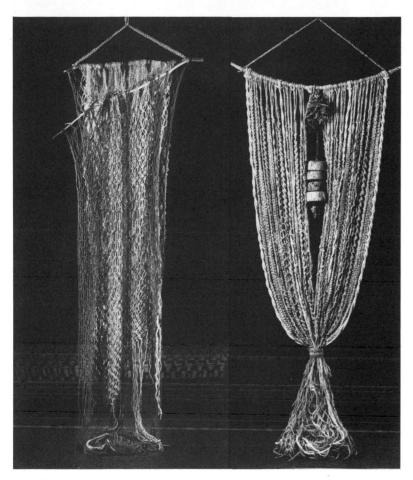

6–68 *Medicine Man.* 96 × 32 inches, by Dina Barzel; photo courtesy of the artist.

6–65. *The Nets Are Empty,* knotted jute, wool, and horsehair with woven background, by Else Regensteiner; photo by John W. Rosenthal.

6–66. *Gem of the Sea,* hanging with fishermen's cork and seaweed, by Else Regensteiner; photo by John W. Rosenthal.

6–67. Knotted hanging by Stana Coleman; photo by Robert Fields.

6–69. *Guards,* 8 × 14 feet, by Dina Barzel; photo courtesy of the artist.

REFERENCES

Atwater, Mary Meigs. *Byways in Handweaving.* New York: Macmillan, 1968.

Birrell, Verla. *The Textile Arts.* New York: Schocken, 1973.

Burnham, Harold B. and Dorothy K. *Keep Me Warm One Night, Early Handweaving in Eastern Canada.* References to Beiderwand on pages 326 and 327. Toronto: Univ. of Toronto Press, 1972.

Chamberlain, Marcia and Crockett, Candace. *Beyond Weaving.* New York: Watson-Guptill, 1974. Includes information on knotless netting, braiding, cardweaving, wrapping and coiling.

Christopher, F. J. *Basketry.* New York: Dover, 1952.

Collingwood, Peter. *The Techniques of Rug Weaving.* New York; Watston-Guptill, 1969.

Crockett, Candace. *Card Weaving.* New York: Watson-Guptill, 1973.

Davison, Marguerite Porter. *A Handweaver's Pattern Book.* Swarthmore, Pa., 1951.

Davison, Mildred and Mayer-Thurman, Christa. *Coverlets, A Handbook on the Collection of Woven Coverlets in the Art Institute of Chicago,* 1973.

D'Harcourt, Raoul. *Textiles of Ancient Peru and Their Techniques.* Seattle: Univ. of Washington, 1973.

Emery, Irene. *Primary Structures of Fabrics.* Washington, D.C.: Textile Museum, 1966.

Groff, Russell E. *Card Weaving or Tablet Weaving.* McMinnville, Ore.: Robin and Russ Hand Weavers, 1969.

Harvey, Virginia I. *The Techniques of Basketry.* New York: Van Nostrand Reinhold, 1974.

James, Ona. "Swivel, Variations for a Four-Harness Loom," *Handweaver and Craftsman,* Vol. 14, No. 4, Fall, 1963.

Krevitsky, Nik and Lois Ericson. *Shaped Weaving.* New York: Van Nostrand Reinhold, 1974. Simple needle- and finger-weaving techniques.

Mayer-Thurman, Christa. *Masterpieces of Western Textiles from the Art Institute of Chicago,* 1969.

NanKivell, Joice (Mrs. J. M. Loch). *Prosforion-Uranopolous, Rugs and Dyes.* Istanbul (American Board Publications Department): J. M. Loch, 1964.

Regensteiner, Else. *The Art of Weaving.* New York: Van Nostrand Reinhold, 1970. A complete weaving bibliography may be found in this book, as well as detailed instructions on basic weaving.

Rossbach, Ed. *Baskets As Textile Art.* New York: Van Nostrand Reinhold, 1973.

Snow, Marjorie and William. *Step by Step Tablet Weaving.* New York: Golden Press, 1973.

Specht, Sally and Sandra Rawlings. *Creating with Card Weaving.* New York: Crown, 1973.

Tacker, Harold and Sylvia. *Band Weaving.* New York: Van Nostrand Reinhold, 1974. Contains information on inkle weaving, cardweaving, and other portable-loom techniques.

Tidball, Harriet. *Weaving Inkle Bands,* Monograph 27. Craft & Hobby, Shuttle Craft Guild, 1969.

West, Rebecca. *Black Lamb & Gray Falcon.* New York: Viking, 1941.

Wilson, Jean and Burhen, Jan. *Weaving You Can Wear.* New York: Van Nostrand Reinhold, 1973.

INDEX